PRAISE FOR
Do It Afraid

"When Kent speaks, you listen. When he writes, you read. God has filled him with so much wisdom and insight, it's inspiring. I am so blessed to call him a friend, mentor, and brother in Christ. Do It Afraid is a must-read for anyone trying to get the most out of their life, marriage, and faith."

Ben Roethlisberger, two-time NFL Super Bowl champion quarterback, Pittsburgh Steelers

---

"What is holding you back from living your life to the full? Based on his own journey, Kent Chevalier addresses the underlining sabotage that most of us have to face to get to where we want to go: fear. Within the pages of Do It Afraid you will find heartfelt honesty, endless encouragement, and a practical pathway that will move you off the sidelines and on to the frontlines of fulfilling your God-given purpose. I've watched and walked with Kent in his journey, and now, through Do It Afraid, he wants to walk with you through yours!"

Dave Buehring, founder and president, Lionshare Leadership Group

---

"Kent has been a colleague and good friend of mine for over a decade now. I appreciate his experience, strength, and the insights that he has graciously shared in this book. His knowledge and experience will undoubtedly add value."

Clint Hurdle, National League Manager of the Year (2013); 17-year Major League manager, Colorado Rockies and Pittsburgh Pirates

"Fear is a national pandemic. We have more insurance policies, seat belts, helmets, phobias, and meds than any generation on any corner of the planet.
Kent gives us a great road map of how to overcome fear in key life situations. I find his writing, vulnerability, and instruction to be inspiring and incredibly helpful."

Brian Tome, senior pastor, Crossroads Church

"Everyone has or had something in their life that has kept them from reaching their full potential. In a lot of cases, that something is fear. Fear of failure, fear of others' opinions, fear of letting someone down. In Do It Afraid, Kent provides biblical, informative, and strategic ways to help those who are facing a choice in their life to take action, so God can fulfill His purposes through their lives."

Alex Highsmith, NFL outside linebacker, Pittsburgh Steelers

"Kent's message of Do It Afraid gave me courage to keep moving forward when I wanted to quit most, and gave our family the confidence we needed to step into the most purposeful season of our lives!"

Davin Salvagno, best-selling author of Thieves of Purpose and cofounder of The Purpose Summit

---

"With refreshingly raw vulnerability, my longtime friend shares his unique experience discerning the will of God throughout his life. Wisdom is often obtained the hard way, and not only is Kent unafraid to reveal his less glamorous moments, but he's eager to encourage and equip us with insight gained and practical lessons learned along the way. Do It Afraid will prepare you to take your next steps into an unknown future, with the confidence that God is with you."

Aaron Shust, Christian singer/songwriter

"Not only in this book, but in life, Kent shows the ultimate display of what following Jesus is all about. He's a true leader of men."

Miles Killebrew, two-time NFL Pro Bowler, Pittsburgh Steelers

---

"Many writers publish an extended blog post, dressed up as a book. This is not one of them. Kent pairs his journey dealing with the fear that drives many of us with practical steps that you can start today. They're not complicated but essential to hearing the voice of God as we make decisions, big and small. Jump in, and "do it afraid." See where God leads you. It led Kent somewhere he never expected."

Sonya Bearson, former national broadcast journalist and host of the Lionshare Leadership Group podcast *Wisdom Unlocked: The Ways of God.*

"A new generation is seeking righteousness and truth today around the world. It is humbling to witness their massive pursuit. Do it Afraid not only gives us an understanding of that pursuit but also a very clear resource in Christ to serve it with. Kent Chevalier has been blessed with the wisdom to communicate into this pursuit because he chose long ago to truly lay his life down for it."

Matt Geppert, president, Pittsburgh Leadership Foundation and SEAPC

"Kent Chevalier has given us more than a memoir— he's given us a roadmap. His L.E.A.P. framework transformed how I think about making fear-filled decisions. This book doesn't eliminate fear; it teaches you how to move forward with it. Every leader facing a crossroads needs this."

Jacob Brown, speaker, author, and coach

"What sticks out to me most in Kent and Erica's journey is how you can see God forming them long before He brought them to the Steelers. Kent is honest about fear, disappointment, and those moments when God quietly pushes you forward anyway. The discipleship reflections that follow are simple, solid, and profoundly helpful. If you are struggling with a calling that feels greater than your confidence, this book will meet you right where you are and give you the courage to take the next step."

Preston Poore, author of How Is Greater Than What, speaker, trainer, coach, and former Fortune 100 executive

---

"Kent Chevalier has been a steady guide in my walk with Christ. His honesty is real, his words are direct, and his heart is genuine. Kent leads with courage—never afraid to step into hard conversations—and in doing so, he creates space for others to grow, trust, and move forward in their faith. Do It Afraid reflects the same bold, honest leadership he lives every day."

Cameron Heyward, Walter Payton Man of the Year 2023, seven-time Pro Bowler, Pittsburgh Steelers

---

"One of the most important messages in Do It Afraid is Kent's challenge about our addiction to comfort. We're drawn to it in every area of our lives... our careers, our ministries, our relationships, and even our faith. But here's the truth Kent drives home in this book: if we're going to fulfill God's purposes for us, we're going to have to step out of our comfort zones and face our fears head on. This book doesn't just inspire you to do that, it equips you with biblical and practical steps to actually take the leap."

Alan Hannah, lead pastor, Allegheny Center Alliance Church

"In Do It Afraid, Pastor Kent provides a challenging reminder that the calling for the believer is not to a life of safety but to a life of surrender to God. Through transparency and authenticity, we are invited into a story of the power of God at work in the lives of this dynamic couple and as a result learn some lessons for our own journey as well. Grounded in Scripture, each page will both challenge and comfort you as you seek to live the life God is calling you towards."

Todd Allen, vice president for diversity affairs, Messiah University

---

"Kent's book is a game changer. His story will inspire you. His heart for the Gospel will encourage you. This book gets my highest recommendation. Go read Do it Afraid now."

Jason Romano, author of Live to Forgive and executive producer of Sports Spectrum

---

"Doing it afraid is a requirement for fulfilling God's plan for our lives. In this book, Kent shows us how to press through our fears and push through to our destinies. This is a message he has been living for the last twenty-plus years I've known him. May it serve as a roadmap for your journey."

Doug Smith, founder and CEO, L3 Leadership

"Do It Afraid is a powerful reminder that great things happen when we step out of our comfort zone, overcome fear, and listen to the unction of the Spirit of God. Kent reassures us that faith takes action. He is a living example. The book is a must-read for those ready to live out their purpose."

Jay Simon, financial advisor

Do It Afraid

UNLEASHING THE COURAGE TO JUMP
INTO YOUR GOD-GIVEN PURPOSE

KENT CHEVALIER

MAISON VERO

Published by Maison Vero
3002 Dow Avenue, Suite 112
Tustin, CA 92780

Copyright © 2026 by Kent Chevalier.

Maison Vero is a professional publishing house that partners with rising authors to bring their thought leadership to the world. By respecting the copyright of an author's intellectual property, you enable Maison Vero and the author to continue publishing exceptional books for years to come. We thank you for supporting the author's copyright by purchasing an authorized edition of this book.

No amount of this book may be reproduced or stored in any format, nor may it be uploaded to any website, database, language-learning model, or other repository, retrieval, or artificial intelligence system without express permission. All rights reserved.

Inquiries may be directed to: Maison Vero, 3002 Dow Avenue, Suite 112, Tustin, CA 92780, or info@graymilleragency.com.

For information about special discounts for bulk purchases, please call (949) 333-4872 or email info@graymilleragency.com.

Maison Vero is a partner brand of The Gray + Miller Agency, a speaking, literary, and talent consortium.

For more information on the talent represented by The Gray + Miller Agency, or to bring any of our thought leaders to your organization or live event, please visit our website at graymilleragency.com

Cover Design: Mike Elwell
Book Design: Mike Elwell

Paperback 978-1-969508-20-2
Hardcover 978-1-969508-21-9

DEDICATION

For Erica.
Look at what God has done.
Thanks for jumping with me!

TABLE OF **Contents**

FOREWORD: MIKE TOMLIN — XIII

PART 1: JUMP WITH FEAR

Part 1: Jump WITH Fear — 2
1. Fear Has a Name — 7
2. Comfortable — 14
3. Needles in the Nest — 29
4. There's Gotta Be Another Way — 43
5. Lessons from a Nest — 60
6. When God Shows Up and Shows Off! — 65
7. Do It Afraid — 69

PART 2: L.E.A.P. BEFORE YOU JUMP

Part 2: L.E.A.P. Before You Jump — 80
8. Let God Lead — 81
9. Express Your Fears — 87
10. Ask For Wisdom — 96
11. P.R.A.Y. Through It — 104
12. Prayer Runway — 113
13. Read God's Word — 120
14. Active Waiting — 133
15. Yield to God's Call — 143

CONCLUSION

Conclusion — 154
ACKNOWLEDGMENTS — 157
ABOUT THE AUTHOR — 160

Foreword

MIKE TOMLIN
FORMER HEAD COACH OF THE PITTSBURGH STEELERS

When you spend your life in a locker room, you learn pretty quickly that football is about a lot more than X's and O's. It's about people. It's about pressure, purpose, resilience, accountability, and belief. It's about how men carry themselves when the lights are bright—and when no one is watching. In that space, where preparation meets adversity, and talent meets expectation, Pastor Kent Chevalier has been a steady, trusted, and deeply meaningful presence for the Pittsburgh Steelers.

Kent, affectionately known as PK, has served as our team chaplain for years, but titles don't fully capture impact. When you hear the word "chaplain," people sometimes think quiet and distant—someone who exists on the margins or speaks softly from the back of the room. That has never been PK. He has never made his role about commanding attention or standing in front of the room with answers to every question. His influence comes from something far more powerful: consistency, authenticity, and care. He shows up. He listens. He speaks truth when it's needed or offers silence if that's what the moment calls for. In a profession built on noise, he understands the value of stillness.

In the NFL, the margin for error is razor-thin. Every player, coach, and staff member who walks through our facility is carrying something—

expectations, family responsibilities, personal struggles, injuries, doubts, and dreams. He understands that football players are still men. He doesn't reduce people to roles, stats, or contracts. He sees the whole person, the individual, and that perspective matters more than most people realize.

One of the things I respect most about PK is his understanding of team culture. He doesn't attempt to impose anything foreign onto it. He honors it. He respects the traditions, values, and standards that define the Black and Gold. He understands that our locker room is diverse — men from different beliefs, upbringings, and experiences — and he navigates that diversity with wisdom and humility. His door is open to everyone, and no one feels judged for walking through it.

His ministry is built on trust, and trust takes time. It's earned by being present on ordinary days, not just in moments of crisis. It's earned by keeping confidence and leading with contagious courage, as PK would say. Players trust and know that conversations with PK stay with PK. Coaches know that his counsel is thoughtful and grounded. That kind of credibility can't be demanded — it can only be demonstrated.

In professional football, we talk a lot about preparation. PK prepares people for life. He reminds us that wins and losses, while important, are not finite. He helps players navigate success without losing perspective and handle disappointment without losing hope. He encourages accountability without condemnation and growth without shame. That balance is rare, and it's invaluable.

I've watched young players lean on him as they transition into the league, learning how to balance newfound attention and responsibility. I've seen veteran players seek him out during pivotal moments in their careers — times of transition, uncertainty, or reflection. I've seen coaches and staff do the same. His impact is not limited to Sunday afternoons; it extends into homes, families, and futures.

What makes him especially effective is that he understands leadership. He knows that leadership isn't about control — it's about influence.

It's about serving others, setting an example, and being willing to walk alongside people rather than ahead of them. That philosophy aligns closely with how we strive to lead within this organization. He reinforces our emphasis on discipline, character, and purpose without ever needing to say a word about football.

PK also understands adversity, and that understanding gives his words power. He doesn't offer clichés or easy answers. He acknowledges pain, struggle, and doubt as real parts of being human. At the same time, he consistently points people toward hope, responsibility, and faith. He challenges men to be better husbands, fathers, teammates, and people — not for recognition, but because it's the right thing to do.

The Steelers are built on a strong foundation of values that have endured for generations. PK has been a steward of those values in a quiet but powerful way. He reinforces the idea that how we live matters just as much as how we perform. That message resonates in a league where careers can be short, and identities can easily become tied to a number on a jersey.

This book is an extension of who he is and what he stands for. It reflects his heart for people, his commitment to faith, and his belief that purpose is discovered through service and integrity. Whether you are a football fan, a leader, a parent, or someone searching for direction, you will find wisdom here that applies far beyond the gridiron.

I am grateful for Kent Chevalier — not just for what he does, but for who he is. He has been a blessing to this team, to this organization, and to countless individuals who may never appear on a stat sheet, but whose lives have been shaped by his presence. The Steelers are better because he is part of our family.

As you read these pages, know that they come from a man who lives what he believes. PK's voice has mattered in our locker room, and it will matter to you as well. I'm proud to call him our chaplain, our friend, and a trusted partner in the work of building men of character — on and off the field.

PART 1

Jump WITH Fear

PART 1: JUMP WITH FEAR

I was afraid to jump. I so badly wanted to, but my brain had me convinced it wasn't safe. My heart was beating so fast I could feel the thumping in my temples. As I moved closer to the edge of the cliff, I could see those who had already made the leap perched on the rocks below, showing me exactly where to jump.

It was a forty-foot drop and below, the river carved a ten-foot-wide natural landing zone. You had to time your run perfectly, leaping far enough to clear the jagged rocks lining the gorge, yet not so far that you'd overshoot the deep water waiting to catch you.

My knees were shaking. I contemplated backing out, but peer pressure and the thrill of adventure got the best of me that day.

Even though I was afraid, I jumped anyway.

I took several steps back and then took off running. I planted my foot and leapt with a wild scream.

I felt like I was in the air forever.

My mind went wild with all kinds of crazy thoughts. Did I jump out too far? Did I not jump far enough? Why was it taking so long for me to hit the water? Am I going to hit the rocks and be paralyzed—or worse, die? Why did I do this?

Smack! My feet hit and I plunged into the deep, cold water. It took my breath away.

I kicked hard and swam toward the surface. As I neared the top, I could hear my buddies shouting. "Way to go, man!" "That was awesome!" "You did it, Kent!" I paddled over to the edge of the rocks laughing, a great feeling of pride in my chest.

I did it. I made the jump!

I'd never felt more alive in my life!

I want that for you — for your faith, marriage, family, vocation, mission, and God-given purpose in this life! I want you to know and experience the adventure God is calling you to and the purpose for which He has created you to live. But here's the thing... it will require you to embrace the fear of the unknown and take a leap of faith.

As a pastor for twenty-seven years now, I am convinced that many followers of Jesus have settled for a version of Christianity that stays on top of the cliff. It's safe up there. It's more comfortable. There's no risk.

But I don't want that for you.

I don't want you to settle for an insufficient version of Christianity that doesn't require you to sacrifice for Jesus' mission. I don't want you to buy into a message that all God wants to do is make your life more comfortable. I don't want you to believe in a safe Christianity that is void of risk, failure, and hard lessons.

I want you to jump with me.

I'm not talking about jumping off a cliff in the Adirondacks. Although that'd be awesome if I was eighteen years old again!

I'm inviting you to jump into your God-given purpose!

There is this narrow landing zone where God's call meets your obedience to jump and trust Him with your life. And it's there that you will come alive in ways beyond your imagination.

C'mon!

You know you want to do it. You can feel it in your gut. You dream about it. You can't shake it. You think about it in your free time. If you had all the money in the world, you would do it. You may have even created a plan for it. You know God is calling you to do it, and you'd love to jump, but…

There's something holding you back. Keeping you at the top of the cliff. A comfortable lifestyle.

A family to provide for. A friend's strong opinion. A good position at work. A solid paycheck.

And this is where the fear begins to creep in. It tries to convince you not to jump. It causes your knees to shake.

The fear of change.

The fear of not having enough. The fear of failure.

The fear of rejection. The fear of the unknown.

And I get it. I've been there. I understand. These are legitimate concerns.

However, I want to challenge you. I want to encourage you to count the cost of staying on top of the cliff and not jumping into God's call on your life.

Throughout our journey together, I'll ask you some tough questions.

- Have you ever considered how your way of providing for your family could actually be hindering you and them from experiencing God as Provider?

- Have you given thought to how cultural comfort is actually robbing you of God's gift of holy discomfort?

- Have you ever taken the time to weigh the eternal consequences of saying "no" to God?

You might need to stop reading for a minute and prayerfully consider the questions you just read.

My hope in writing this book is to encourage you to trust God with everything, including your fears. He knows exactly what you're afraid of and why. It's natural! So, embrace that fear, and give it to Him. His calling on your life takes your fears into account.

By sharing my "Do It Afraid" story with you, I hope to inspire you to jump. I want to be for you who my buddies were for me when they jumped before me that day in the Adirondacks. I want to be the guy forty feet below, cheering for you to take a leap of faith into the calling God has on your life.

"Do It Afraid" has become a life mantra for me. In 2019, I was faced with the decision to either jump into a God-sized calling or bow to the thieves of familiarity, security, and comfort. After twenty-two years of serving as a pastor in the local church context, God presented me with a once-in-a-lifetime opportunity, but it came with a massive cost. And I want to tell you that story and how it transpired.

The first part of this book will be a testimony of what God has done in my life. I have taken several leaps of faith in my thirty years of following Jesus, and I will attempt to share the wisdom I've learned along the way. I'd love to say that every time I jumped, I hit the landing zone, but I didn't.

There were hard lessons from jumping too soon and hitting the rocks. I'll be honest with you about my mistakes. I'll share the painful moments that required God's healing while also recounting the incredible life-giving and divine moments.

The second part of this book is the process that Erica and I use to make these types of decisions. We have learned to L.E.A.P. before we jump. I'll take you through a series of practical action steps found in Scripture that we have learned over three decades of following Jesus together. We've learned these powerful lessons from great mentors along the way, and I will share with you the exact Bible-inspired steps we took before we made one of the biggest decisions of our lives.

You were created for a purpose. You were designed to take this leap of faith. God's call on your life is so important. Your "yes" to God is paramount and filled with eternal ramifications.

There are good reasons not to jump, but they're not God reasons.

It's time for you to embrace the fear of the unknown and jump into your God-given purpose.

Do it afraid.

CHAPTER 1

Fear Has a Name

I didn't realize we were poor until I realized we were poor. The collapse of the steel industry in Pittsburgh and the 1982 closing of Crucible Steel Mill in Midland left my dad without a job, scrambling to find work and jumping from job to job for many years. My mom stayed home with my siblings and me, but she eventually had to start watching other kids at our home to help make ends meet.

When I use the term "poor" to describe my circumstances, I cringe. Because compared to global poverty, I was rich. I never missed a meal, and I always had clothes on my back (mostly hand-me-downs from my cousins and yard sale finds). I had a bed to sleep in and a roof over my head. But I also don't want to discount the hard times my parents went through in the '80s and '90s. As a little guy, I remember seeing my mom pay for groceries with food stamps. I vividly remember standing in a government food line with her in Beaver Falls. The awful taste of powdered milk mixed with water is still with me to this day. Gross!

"IOU"

When I was ten years old, I got my first job as a paperboy. If I wanted anything, my parents told me I would have to pay for it myself with the tips I made from going door to door. If you're under the age of thirty, it might surprise you to know that people used to get their world and local news on paper delivered right to their door. Not on their phone. Crazy, I know.

As a paperboy, I collected money from my customers every two weeks for their subscription. I had a little yellow bag with my school mascot "Blackhawk Cougars" logo on it. Inside was cash to make change: a lot of ones, a few fives, and a ten.

One day, I opened my collection bag to find a small, ripped note in my mom's handwriting: "IOU $2 for milk." I was shocked that my mom had to borrow money from me. At that moment, I realized we were poor. In hindsight, I'm sure my mom was probably just short of cash that day, but this IOU impressed something impure onto my heart. It did something to me. An embarrassment washed over me, and I knew from that moment on I didn't want to struggle financially.

I vowed that day I would never be in a financial situation where I had to depend on anyone else—especially my kids—for anything.

I think God took notice that day of the seed of deceit planted in my heart and mind.

It grew as I began to compare who I was and what I could afford to my buddies in school and what they had. The problem was I could never measure up—or keep up.

Money became a fixation for me. I got caught up in wanting what was expensive; the latest fads fueled me. In fifth grade, I had to have a pair of Skidz. Michael Jackson's parachute pants were a necessity. I wanted a Nintendo Entertainment System, so I saved all my paper-route Christmas tips to pay for it. And a Rawlings baseball glove wasn't good enough—I wanted a Mizuno glove.

The problem was this stuff was getting too expensive. My tips weren't cutting it for all the nice things I wanted.

PAIN IN THE "AIR"

I'll never forget my first day of seventh grade. Nike's latest Air Jordan sneakers had come out just in time for the new school year.

Even though I knew we couldn't afford them, I pleaded with my parents day after day. "All of my buddies are going to have the new Jordans! Please!" My begging was always met with the same answer.

"Kent, spending that much on a pair of shoes that will be ruined in a week is a waste of money!"

I countered: "Okay, can I at least get a pair of Nike Airs?" A pair of Nike's weren't good enough; I wanted Nike Airs.

"No, those are still too expensive."

"Fine!," I said. "Can I get a pair of Nike's then?" My mom finally gave in, and we went shopping.

I thought I'd devised a good plan. I picked out a pair of black high-tops with a white swoosh that stretched all the way to the heel where a black Nike above the black swoosh was overlayed on the white plastic. "These are the ones I want, Mom!"

She paid half, and I paid for the rest with my paper-route tips.

The day before school started, I took a black permanent marker and carefully wrote A-I-R under the black swoosh of each shoe. Nobody would even notice.

I was so pumped to wear my new "Nike AIR" shoes on the first day of seventh grade at Highland Middle School! Then I saw all my buddies wearing the new Jordans and I felt inferior.

Funny how a shoe can do that.

At the end of the day, as we all packed up at our lockers, I bent down with one knee on the ground and my foot stretched behind me, focused on pulling my books from my locker.

"Nice shoes, Chevalier!" I looked up to see my "friend" laughing and pointing. He was wearing a pair of new Air Jordans. He then shouted "Everybody! Look at Kent's shoes! He wrote AIR on his Nike's! He's SO POOR he can't even afford Nike Airs!"

I was devastated.

Everyone was laughing at me. I felt like the poorest kid in school.

I was beyond horrified.

I was so angry, but instead of punching my "friend" in the mouth, I slammed my locker and ran away wiping the tears from my eyes, hoping nobody would see me cry.

On the bus ride home, animosity toward my parents brewed. It was *their fault* for not buying me the Air Jordans. It was *their fault* that we were so "poor" in the first place.

I made another vow: I would never be so poor that I couldn't afford nice things for myself and my family.

Now, that seed of financial insecurity grew into a weed. Its roots burrowed deep and wrapped around my heart and mind.

NAMING YOUR FEAR

I have many fears.

A fear of failure — I hate failing.

A fear of change — I know change is constant, but I'm still not a fan.

A fear of disappointing people — I can be known as a people pleaser.

A fear of having a heart attack — My family history points to any day now.

A fear of my wife cheating on me — If you know Erica, you know this is completely irrational.

A fear that you won't like this book — Your approval will validate my success, right?

A fear of my past — If people really knew what happened, I'd be canceled.

A fear of rejection — I like it when everybody likes me.

But if I had to pick one deep-seated fear that really drives me, it would have to be...

The fear of not having enough.

Have you ever done the work to identify a fear that drives you?

Some fears are easy to identify. A fear of snakes. A fear of heights. A fear of public speaking.

But deep-seated fear is harder to recognize. It takes time and hard work to dig in the dirt to understand how that fear first appeared and why that fear is making unknown decisions in the background of your life and ultimately driving you to behave in certain ways.

Sometimes you don't even know what you're afraid of; all you know is you want to avoid whatever is causing you to feel that way. Then you start doing certain things and behaving in certain ways — intentionally or not — to mask the fear.

To begin your journey of embracing the fear of the unknown and jumping into your God-given purpose, you must do the hard work of identifying and naming your fear.

Do me a favor. Do yourself a favor. Take out a sheet of paper right now or open the notes app on your phone. Make the time to do this.

GIVE YOUR FEAR A NAME

Make a list of all the things that cause you fear, even those that seem trivial, like spiders or dogs. (I'm afraid of big dogs because I got bitten so many times as a paper boy!)

Once you get past the obvious external phobias, reflect on what gives you worry and anxious thoughts on a regular basis. Do an honest evaluation of what drives your thoughts and emotions. Maybe turn to your spouse, a mentor, a parent, or a trusted friend for guidance.

Ask yourself, "When I read the title *Do It Afraid*, what holds me back from doing the 'it' I know I want to do? What keeps me from jumping?"

Now that you have your list of fears, pick an internal one. The fear of...

...Losing a relationship

...Disappointing your dad

...Being out of control

...Financial insecurity

...Career uncertainty

Then, try to name that internal fear. It's one thing to identify how a fear makes you feel, but something shifts in our thinking and praying when we give that fear a name.

You can make the name even more personal. I sometimes refer to my driving fear of not having enough as "IOU" to remind me of the seed moment. I could also call it "AIR" and immediately feel the embarrassment in the hallway and the anger on the bus ride.

Go ahead and give it a try. Give your fear a name.

Don't go on to the next chapter until you name at least one fear. Seriously... put the book down.

💡 Key Takeaways

- Internal fears have deep roots that must be traced back and dug up.
- Naming your fear(s) exposes its power and brings it into the light.
- The enemy of your soul will keep compounding your fear(s) in different ways.
- Vows made from fear can drive a wedge in between you and your God-given purpose.

❓ Application Questions

1. Have you ever experienced something that made you feel inferior? Describe it.
2. What are a few of your internal fears that seem to drive you?
3. What name will you give to your fear(s)?

CHAPTER 2

Comfortable

I wouldn't say I dreamed of being rich, but I couldn't bear the thought of being poor. I didn't want to worry about money like my parents did. I didn't want to make decisions based on what wasn't in my bank account. I never cared about what kind of car I drove (and I still don't), but I wanted something dependable. I wasn't interested in a huge home, but I wanted a nice house for my family.

Not rich. Not poor. Comfortable.

Comfort — that was the goal. I wanted a life filled with it, not just for me, but for my family as well.

Many would call that a healthy desire. But for me, the pursuit of comfort almost robbed me of the calling God had for me.

My fear of *not having enough* nearly kept me from jumping into my God-given purpose several times in my adult life. My original "IOU" and "AIR" experiences strengthened into a massive vine that continued to wrap around me and trip me up.

The fear of being poor ruled me. The fear of not being able to afford nice things drove my decisions. And the pressure of not being able to provide enough for my wife wrapped around me so tightly that God's calling on my life felt constantly at odds with this deep-seated fear of not having—or providing—enough.

MINISTRY + MONEY

People don't go into ministry for money. (Okay… some do, but they're rare outliers who prey on the vulnerable.) Most people who worry about not being able to provide for their families don't become pastors or ministry leaders. If money is a driving concern for you, you're probably not headed into ministry.

But I was.

God made that clear to me when I was nineteen years old. But the journey to get there was rough.

I grew up going to church, but I didn't really own my faith. It was more my parents' faith than mine. I managed to be good when church people were watching, but I was a hypocrite when they weren't. I said I was a Christian, but I did a lot of things that I'm not proud of that didn't honor Jesus Christ.

When I got into middle school, the relationship between my dad and me grew rocky. He was very strict, and I rebelled against his church and house rules, but never strayed too far out of line for fear of the painful consequences. During my sophomore year of high school, I headed in a bad direction by getting involved in illegal underage drinking and drug use, so my parents and I agreed it would be a good idea for me to transfer to a Christian school the following year. I thought that would help, but I managed to fall into a crowd that drew me further away from Jesus and closer to mischief.

As graduation approached, I remember feeling trapped. All I wanted was to get out of my dad's house and leave Pittsburgh, but I didn't have that option. I was headed to Geneva College because my mom had the wisdom and foresight to get a job there in food services so I could have a free college education.

I was frustrated about having to attend college in my hometown. It felt like all my buddies had moved on after graduation, leaving me behind. I no longer wanted to attend my parents' church, but my dad insisted. When an opportunity came to attend a youth conference, I resisted — I was too old, and none of my friends were going. Still, my dad made me go.

During the conference, it felt as though every speaker knew my story. At first, I wondered if my parents had contacted them to address the struggles I was facing at home. Now I realize God was using each speaker to speak directly to me. On Thursday night, when one of the speakers shared the good news of Jesus' death on the cross for the forgiveness of my sins, I felt deeply convicted about my choices and the person I had become. That night, I responded to the invitation to receive Christ as my Lord and Savior and committed to following Him for the rest of my life.

I came back home a changed young man.

A few weeks later, I went to Geneva College, unsure what I wanted to do with my life. There I met Rich Grassel my freshman year. He was a part-time professor who taught student ministry classes. He began to disciple me in the ways, character, and mission of Jesus. He also invited me to play my acoustic guitar in the student ministry band at his church.

I watched as Rich made the Bible fun and exciting to those sixth through twelfth grade students. The way he explained the Bible stories helped me grow in my faith. He saw that I was hungry to learn more, and he called out the leadership gift in me. He invited me to lead youth group games. He quickly put me in charge of the sixth-grade boys to lead the small group discussions. He even gave me my first opportunity to preach a message from the Bible to students. I began to look forward to his student ministry every week.

During my sophomore year, I grew closer to Rich. He introduced me to his family. I stayed home with his two elementary-aged sons while he and his wife, Ruth, went out on dates. He invited me over for dinner after church to watch the Pittsburgh Steelers play.

I wanted to be with Rich because he continued to invest in me and invite me to fun things, like Laurelville Mud Weekend (an awesome weekend retreat for sixth through twelfth graders) and Surf City (a week-long camp on the sand dunes of Lake Michigan). He introduced me to the Pittsburgh Youth Network, an intentional community of church student ministry leaders, by inviting me to leadership planning retreats. I was the only college kid in the room of Pittsburgh youth ministry legends. It was in rooms like these that I met guys like Brad Henderson (who would go on to become the president of the Pittsburgh Kids Foundation, chaplain to the Pittsburgh Pirates and Penguins, and Erica's boss) and Scott Stevens (a veteran youth pastor who would eventually become a mentor and my boss).

One day, Rich promised to pay me if I helped him paint the inside of a house. As he taught me how to properly cover floors, tape the walls, paint the edges, and wash the brushes, he turned to me and said, "Kent, I could really see you doing student ministry after college. Have you ever considered that?"

I never had.

We went on to discuss God's calling on my life and how I should consider ministry. What I didn't know was Rich actually got paid to do student ministry. What?

I thought Rich got paid to be a professor at Geneva College. I thought his side business was painting. And I assumed he volunteered at his church. But it turned out he was also paid to lead the student ministry!

I remember thinking, "Wait—student ministry? You get paid to do student ministry? This is a job?" Planning youth group games, giving sermons, eating pizza, and hanging out with students—sign me up. I was hooked.

God was clearly using Rich to call me into a life-long adventure of ministry.

The problem was I didn't realize Rich *had* to work three jobs because ministry alone couldn't pay him enough to make ends meet. He painted to help cover the bills—not because he wanted to, but because he had to. His purpose and passion were to train the next generation of youth pastors, but that calling didn't come with enough income to support this family. I respect him so much for doing whatever it took.

But once I realized this, I was torn.

I wanted a role in ministry, but I also wanted financial comfort. The deep-seated fear of my "IOU" and "AIR" experiences started to choke out student ministry as my possible purpose and calling. I admired what Rich had and wanted to follow that path, but I still longed for comfort. I knew I didn't want to face the same financial struggles he and my parents went through.

MARRIAGE + MINISTRY + MONEY

I'll never forget the first time I saw Erica. I was in Geneva College's gymnasium shooting hoops when she walked in with her cheerleading squad. My sister, Shannon, was her captain, so she did me a solid and introduced me. A few weeks later, she and I began to talk.

One night after a student fellowship, I noticed Erica and her friends down on their hands and knees searching for something in the grass. I went over and asked what they were looking for.

Erica replied, "I lost the charm my dad gave me."

I glanced down, and right beside my foot was the charm.

"Is this it?"

"Yes!" she screamed, and this was the beginning of our relationship.

As Erica and I dated through college, it became increasingly clear God was calling us toward marriage and a life of full-time ministry. We served together in student ministry, and beginning our junior year, I worked on campus as the field house manager while also earning a small stipend—$200 a month—as a part-time youth director at nearby church. I saved every bit of it to buy a ring by spring.

Erica and I got engaged during our junior year on Easter Sunday in 1998.

Our senior year was a whirlwind of decisions and transitions. Erica lined up a job after college with Deloitte & Touche as a staff auditor. I was taking a full-time load of Bible and ministry classes while working part-time as a church youth director. Rich had also helped me secure another part-time student ministry role at a local Pittsburgh church with the promise of becoming full-time after graduation.

I was insanely busy, but I was doing what I had to do to provide for our future— just like I saw my parents and Rich do. I had surrendered to the idea that ministry might mean financial struggle, but I was still determined to make my life with Erica as comfortable as possible.

We got married two weeks after college graduation and both started working immediately after our honeymoon. And like most young, newly married couples, we struggled to pay off student loans and make ends meet.

My first full-time job was Christ Church at Grove Farm's youth director. I was paid an annual salary of $23,000 in 1999. And again, compared to global statistics, I was rich—but my reality was that I couldn't even afford to live in the community where the church was located. If it hadn't been for Erica's salary and a precious church couple who rented a house to us for half of what they could've charged, we wouldn't have been able to live anywhere near the church.

Looking back, Erica and I were off to a great start, but there was always this twinge in my heart that it still wasn't enough.

That twinge was pride. The truth was, we had enough. In fact, we had plenty—but my fear of not having enough hindered me from being content in our new life together.

My God-given purpose for ministry was at war with my desire for comfort. Not rich. Not poor. Comfortable.

TIME TO START A FAMILY

Erica and I wanted to be young parents. We were two years into our marriage, and by then, Erica was serving as the full-time assistant to the treasurer at the same church where I was the youth director. The church grew rapidly in those early years, and our entire life became intertwined with it. The youth ministry staff and volunteers became our friends. We were at church events constantly. We were having a blast. The youth ministry was exploding with growth, and we felt ready to grow our own family.

We were thrilled when Erica got pregnant, though the first three months brought awful morning sickness. We began talking about Erica reducing her hours to part-time once the baby was born. We still needed her to work because we wouldn't be able to live comfortably without her salary.

That's when things got interesting. Erica and I were both traveling with a national youth ministry that held events in different cities to introduce students to Jesus. We'd then drive back (sometimes 12–16 hours through the night) and make it home just in time to run the church youth ministry programs.

We knew this pace wouldn't be sustainable once we had our first child, so we both decided to pull back from traveling. After all, we were hired to work for the local church, not the traveling youth ministry. The problem was that the national youth ministry was located on the same property as our church. We shared the same offices. We shared some of the same staff. We were deeply intertwined.

When I communicated our decision to no longer travel, it wasn't well received. My boss and coworkers weren't happy with our decision, and things at the church took a turn. We knew we were at a crossroads.

It was time for me to start looking for another position in youth ministry, which meant Erica would also need to find a different job after the baby was born.

Reluctantly, I began the search.

I privately looked everywhere I knew to look in Pittsburgh. I explored church staff openings online. I made phone calls to local friends within the Pittsburgh Youth Network. I told them to keep it quiet because if I couldn't find another job, I'd have to stay. I thought if the word got out I was looking to leave, I'd be fired.

There were no full-time youth ministry job openings anywhere in the Pittsburgh region. The part-time positions that did exist simply couldn't provide enough to support a family.

During our secret search, Erica gave birth to our first daughter, Madalyn. We were over the moon—officially a family of three.

How in the world would I be able to provide for my growing family? The pressure to provide was building up on my shoulders.

While Erica was on maternity leave, things became extremely awkward for me at the church. Leadership was not happy with our decision. Shared staff didn't know how to navigate the tension. Secret meetings were held about me. The stress was becoming too much, and I knew I had to leave. So, I had to covertly broaden my search for another youth ministry job beyond the Pittsburgh area.

My boss didn't know I was searching. Our extended family didn't know we were looking.

And our youth staff and volunteers had no idea what was going on.

I applied for three youth ministry openings: one in Connecticut, one in Detroit, and one in Baltimore.

Leveraging Erica's maternity leave, we secretly flew to Connecticut first and interviewed. We knew right away that we were not the right fit for that church. Our vision for student ministry did not match their vision.

The following week, we boarded a flight to Detroit. Madalyn was six weeks old. As we sat on the plane before takeoff, Erica said to me, "I'll go with you on this interview, but I won't be moving to Detroit." She didn't want to leave Pittsburgh — neither did I.

On a Friday night, we met with the executive pastor, Rick, and his wife. Our conversation over dinner was enjoyable and easy. We talked for a couple hours at the restaurant as Madalyn slept in her car seat. At the end of our time, Rick handed me a small book, *A Tale of Three Kings* by Gene Edwards. He suggested I look it over for my interview with the senior pastor the next morning.

I was completely put off by this. We had less than twelve hours before meeting with him, and I'd planned to spend most of that time sleeping. Now I had to read this book instead!

It was late when we returned to the hotel. Madalyn was restless but Erica finally got her to sleep and dozed off beside her. I switched on the desk light and cracked open the book — with a bad attitude. Little did I know God was about to crack open my heart.

I don't have words to describe what happened as I began reading *A Tale of Three Kings*. God met me in the darkness of that hotel room. He reached into my chest and gently illuminated every place I had fallen short. He highlighted my pride and arrogance. He illuminated my temper. He showed me where I participated in slander and gossip. My sin was so palpable in that moment as God stripped my heart open. With every page I turned of that powerful little book, God was doing a massive work in me.

I wept quietly, not wanting to wake my wife and daughter.

I finished the entire book—I couldn't put it down. That hotel room became holy ground.

It was brutal and beautiful.

Brutal because God was digging deep within me, exposing my sin and convicting my heart.

Beautiful because, in that same depth, He met me with forgiveness. He washed me clean.

I was physically and emotionally exhausted as I clicked off the desk lamp and climbed into bed. A few hours after I shut my eyes, Madalyn opened hers and let us know it was time to wake up.

We spent Saturday with Pastor Randy Tomko and met the incredible staff of Rockpointe Community Church after the services on Sunday. It was a professional and spiritual gauntlet of an interview, and we loved it.

On our flight home Sunday afternoon, Erica leaned over and admitted, "I already miss them."

She started the weekend off keen on never leaving Pittsburgh; now she wondered if God was telling us to go to Detroit.

Later that week, Randy offered me the youth pastor job. The salary was a slight improvement from what I was making in Pittsburgh. That "raise" felt good.

Erica and I prayed.

The next week I canceled the interview with the church in Baltimore and accepted the offer from Rockpointe.

We told our immediate family. They were... devastated. We were taking their first granddaughter and niece away. Up until that point, none of our families had ever left Pittsburgh.

We told our boss and our youth ministry staff. That didn't go well. Our boss was mad and disappointed because we had secretly interviewed. Our staff was sad and had to navigate the fallout between the local church staff and national youth ministry staff. It was awkward for everyone.

We told our close friends — because we were all on the same staff at this point, they questioned if they should leave too.

We put our house on the market. It was not a good time to sell.

We said goodbye to our Pittsburgh church family and friends. That was painful — but we knew we were meant to go.

A few weeks later, we packed up our unsold house and moved to Detroit.

MULTIPLE MOVES + MISTAKES

We moved into a two-bedroom apartment sight unseen. That was our first mistake.

Even though we lived only six miles from the church building, we didn't realize the traffic patterns would cause my commute to be thirty to forty-five minutes in each direction.

Our second mistake was not realizing the cost-of-living difference between Pittsburgh and Detroit. We figured we'd get to Detroit and then explore where we'd want to buy a house.

It was incredibly expensive to live in the Metro Detroit area at the time. We looked at houses in our youth pastor price range, and our real estate agent showed us a few dilapidated shacks. We quickly realized that we could not afford to buy a comfortable house.

We learned that lesson the hard way.

After three months, we moved to a different apartment that was smaller but closer with less of a commute and traffic.

Meanwhile, our house in Pittsburgh still hadn't sold.

Rockpointe's leadership was so generous— they helped us cover our Pittsburgh mortgage while we covered our Detroit rent with Erica's part-time job. My embarrassment and stress grew. I didn't feel like I was pulling my weight as the provider for my family.

There I was, a twenty-five-year-old husband and dad, and I wasn't doing my job—providing a comfortable life for my family. I was doing the very thing I vowed I would never do—be in a financial situation where I would have to depend on anyone else (other than myself) or so poor I couldn't afford nice things for myself and my family. Now, my daughter was wearing hand-me-downs from other church kids and my wife was cutting coupons for baby food.

I felt like I was failing. As a husband. As a dad. As a pastor. As a man.

Have you ever felt like that? It's awful, isn't it?

I was afraid we were going to have to move back to Pittsburgh. I began to think taking this job in Detroit was a regrettable mistake.

What had I done?

ANOTHER BABY + ANOTHER MOVE

A few months later, Erica started to not feel well. After drawing Erica's blood, the doctor met with her. She slid a sheet of paper across the desk that read, "Pregnancy positive."

Madalyn was only nine months old! Erica and I had just started talking about when we would have a second child.

Erica absorbed the wonderful news and drove straight from the doctor to my office.

Maddie was bouncing in her farm-themed baby bouncer, and Erica shut the door behind her with a concerned look on her face. I thought something was wrong with her health.

Then she shared the news.

I was shocked but excited. We both cried tears of joy.

As the reality of a second baby settled in, the weight of financial responsibility settled back on my shoulders. How in the world was I going to provide for this precious soul? Now there would be four of us in that tiny apartment.

To say I was stressed was an understatement.

Kalea came into our family. She was awesome! We adored her. We were a happy family of four—two daughters under two. We moved Maddie into a big girl's bed and put the crib in our small bedroom. Things were beginning to look up in our little apartment. Things were also beginning to get very crowded.

No one was comfortable. I knew we needed to move again.

When Kalea was born, we had only lived in Michigan for eleven months. We now had two daughters and two mortgages, and I began to wonder if we'd have to move back to Pittsburgh.

If we couldn't sell the Pittsburgh house soon, we'd have to move back. Surely Rockpointe would not be able to cover our Pittsburgh mortgage for the foreseeable future.

I shared my concern with Randy, and he assured me that Rockpointe would stick by our side and cover the Pittsburgh mortgage for a little while longer.

Talk about grace. Talk about sacrificial generosity. We didn't deserve that, but we were so grateful.

Fifteen months after our move to Metro Detroit, we finally sold our Pittsburgh house. What a relief.

We learned how God uses His church to provide in trying times.

We owe so much to our Rockpointe church family. They became our family away from our family. We learned so much about the power and depth of Christian community. We discovered the importance of lowering your guard and trusting the people God puts into your path.

Six months after Kalea was born, we moved into a town home just minutes from the church. Maddie had her own room, and Kalea had a nursery. Erica and I enjoyed a spacious master bedroom with a small balcony. The finished basement became a girls' playroom. There was a community pool and a large shared green space.

This was more like it! Now we were comfortable.

💡 Key Takeaways

- Seeking comfort can rob you of fulfilling your God-given dream.
- Following God's call will cost you, sometimes financially, geographically, and moving away from family.
- God will provide everything you need, not necessarily what you want. What you want might not be what you really need.
- Surround yourself with trusted mentors who will speak God's truth into your life.

❓ Application Questions

1. What is choking out your calling and God-given purpose?
2. Have you ever had a "holy ground" moment where God was convicting and calling you? Describe it.
3. What mistakes have you made that God used to point you towards your purpose?
4. Has anyone ever had to bail you out of a mistake? What did that experience do to your pride or ego?

CHAPTER 3

Needles in the Nest

Just when my family got comfortable, I started to feel uncomfortable. Something began to shift in me — I couldn't put my finger on it.

I was nearing the end of my ninth year of student ministry when Pastor Scott Stevens called me from Pittsburgh. He would take me out to lunch every so often to teach me the "tricks of the trade" as a veteran youth pastor with a large student ministry. Over time, he became a trusted mentor — someone I invited to speak into my life. After we moved, he called regularly to check in and see how I was doing.

On this particular call, he shared that he'd taken a role at North Way Christian Community, a large church in Pittsburgh where some of my extended family attended.

He told me they were looking to hire a teaching pastor to also work with the young adults, and wondered if I would be interested in meeting with Dr. Jay Passavant the next time Erica and were in town. I knew we were headed back for Easter, and Erica agreed I'd at least explore the opportunity.

I met with Pastor Jay who cast a vision for the church and the teaching pastor role. He told me that North Way was preparing to build a larger sanctuary because the church was growing so quickly. As he looked out his office window at the property where it would sit, he described the scale of the new building. While all of it sounded amazing, I knew in my gut that I was not the person for this role. What I had learned to love at Rockpointe was the intimacy of community, and this role and church seemed to be too big for me at that time.

Although I didn't get the offer to move forward in the search process, it felt good that Scott thought I should be considered.

It sparked something in me.

As I entered my tenth year of student ministry, I started to feel like I couldn't keep up with my students. As a young dad of two energetic daughters, I cherished my sleep and loathed youth ministry all-nighters. The upcoming fall retreat felt more like a chore this time around.

I dreamed about stepping into different ministry roles. Maybe I'd lead worship. I wrote worship songs and we sang them during church services. I'd been given an opportunity to preach in "big church" and I genuinely enjoyed it. Maybe I would become a teaching pastor at Rockpointe — or somewhere else.

At twenty-nine, I began to experience what Dave Buehring calls "needles in the nest." This is a concept of getting uncomfortable with your environment, discerning through circumstances, thoughts, or feelings that God is preparing you to fly away from the nest. I met Dave at a youth camp early in our time at Rockpointe, and he quickly became a mentor and trusted voice in my life.

It was nice in the Rockpointe nest. It was cozy and safe there.

But, I could tell my time in student ministry was ending. I also knew I didn't want to leave. We loved our church!

Maybe we could plant a church just like Rockpointe. I could lead it.

I spoke with Randy about what I was wrestling with. He wasn't surprised. He'd seen this pattern before with others. He also assured me that Rockpointe was not in the position to plant a new church because we'd just taken on a new building project.

Randy was encouraging and urged me to take some time away to fast and pray.

He even helped me arrange a cabin in the middle of the woods.

I took my Bible, my guitar, my journal, and some grape juice.

The truth was I had never fasted before. I didn't really know what I was doing.

I worshiped and prayed on an empty belly. I was expectant. I read Scripture. I got really honest with God about my fears, doubts, and questions. I wrote in my journal about knowing my time in youth ministry was ending. I wrote that this probably meant another move, and I didn't want that. I reached a point of gut-level honesty: I did not want to go, but I would if that was what God was calling me to do. Not my will but Yours be done.

I was afraid of what was next, and I didn't even know what that was. I asked God to be very clear with me about what I was supposed to do.

That was November 2005. The cold seeped in as the temperature dropped. I tried to coax a fire in the fireplace, but the wood was wet—and I'm no Boy Scout. Smoke filled the entire cabin. I opened the windows to clear the room and began looking for the thermostat to turn on the heat, but I couldn't find it anywhere. I wandered over to a box mounted on the wall and opened it, discovering it was the fuse box. On the inside of the little door, stamped inside a black rectangle, were the words "Made in Pittsburgh.".

Have you ever had a moment when time stood still? Have you ever had a moment where you could tell that God was speaking directly into your circumstance? Have you ever felt like you were standing on holy ground?

The words "Made in Pittsburgh" hit me like a sudden, profound punch to the chest. My body warmed, and my heart was fixed on that city.

That smoky cabin became my sanctuary.

I had just spent several hours worshiping God, reading the Bible, and telling Him I'd go wherever He wanted to send me. Now there was a profound sense in my spirit that we were going back to Pittsburgh.

When? I didn't know. Where? I didn't know.

What church? I didn't know.

I never found the thermostat that night. But I curled up in some blankets and fell asleep on the couch knowing God had given me His direction.

The cabin was freezing, but my heart was on fire!

The next day I drove home to tell Erica about God's clear direction for us.

A few days later, I told Randy about my cabin experience. With wisdom, he counseled me to wait and not yet begin a search for ministry jobs in Pittsburgh.

He was teaching me a big lesson about waiting for God's timing.

God's timing is just as important as His direction.

THE CALL TO PLANT

A week later, a call came from a college friend, an assistant pastor of a church with a vision to plant churches in the Pittsburgh area over the coming year. He'd been praying about who would lead these plants and couldn't stop thinking about Erica and me, though unsure we'd even be interested.

Was this God's direction and timing or what?

I was interested in learning more. Could this be the "Made in Pittsburgh" call?

I shared the potential job opportunity with Randy. He gave me time off to visit our families for Christmas. During that trip, we were invited to meet with the lead pastor and the rest of the church staff.

We all hit it off! God seemed to be brewing something special.

The lead pastor followed up a couple weeks later to gauge our interest in joining the church plant team. He would send us through a church planting assessment process to see if we were ready.

The results revealed that Erica and I were Level 5 Leaders, qualified to plant a new church. I apparently had what it would take to be the lead pastor of a new church.

That gave us confidence.

But that confidence didn't last long. At the Church Planting Assessment Center, I learned I would have to raise my salary—and not just mine, but the entire team.

I was not a fan of that! I tried hard to not let my fear come through. My "IOU" vine began to tighten its grip.

As a young husband and dad, I didn't think it would be wise to be dependent on other people (outside my church) for my salary.

However, there was a financial model the church planting group had perfected to do this. In the first year, I would have to raise 100 percent of my salary as the church got off the ground. In the second year, I would raise 75 percent, and the new church would cover 25 percent of my salary. In the third year, I would raise 50 percent, and the church would cover 50 percent. In the fourth year, I would raise 25 percent, and the church would cover 75 percent. In the fifth year, the church would be able to sustain my salary moving forward.

They assured me that if we had any trouble raising our salary the church planting organization and the planting church would cover us. It was a "safety net."

Erica and I discussed this opportunity at length. It was a crucial decision.

We prayed for wisdom. We talked it over with our close friends and mentors. But no one else knew what we were considering.

In our waiting, God seemed to be confirming this direction. People who didn't know we were praying about this told us to consider planting a church someday. It was wild!

We became convinced that God was telling us to plant this church in Pittsburgh.

While I wasn't a fan of fundraising, I couldn't deny that God seemed to be in it. The needles in the nest were internally fussing me.

Could I really trust God to provide for my family? Could we handle another out-of-state move? Would I be able to raise my salary? Would I be able to swallow my pride and move in with Erica's parents while this church got up and off the ground?

None of this would be comfortable.

We had a good thing at Rockpointe. I didn't want to leave. But I knew it was time to go.

We communicated our decision to Randy. He was supportive. We told the staff and the church. It was heartbreaking.

We told our families and Pittsburgh friends. They were stoked!

It was bittersweet.

It was time to leave the nest, time to fly. But God knew it was time for us to fall.

THE CRASH OF THE CHURCH PLANT

We moved all our stuff into storage in May 2006 and moved in with Pappy and Nana. It was humbling but only temporary.

We were going to plant the church in a local movie theater in October, so we had four months to find a house, fundraise, build a core team, and launch this new church.

Our faith was strong, and the calling was clear. Until my first staff meeting.

When we left Detroit, I was coming back to Pittsburgh to be the lead pastor of a new church plant. When I got there, I learned I would be a campus pastor within a new structure of a multi-site church. I didn't even know what that meant, and it didn't feel very pastoral or professional to find out with the rest of the staff.

Huge red flag.

The vision of the church had drastically changed in the span of a couple months with no conversation.

I felt belittled. Misled. Even betrayed.

I was furious, but what could I do?

I had no choice but to move forward with this new vision.

Erica and I bought a house six weeks after moving in with her parents. We had this moving thing down by that point — four moves in five years. We were excited to put down roots and dreamed about serving this community for many years.

I met with my new staff: a part-time kids ministry director, a part-time worship director, a part-time production director, and a full-time assistant pastor. We were all committed to raising our salaries to launch this new church.

We found a small storefront that became our offices and a smaller weekly gathering space. We ordered portable church equipment to take back and forth to the movie theater where services would be held.

We began to build our core team. We hosted interest meetings. We sent out marketing mailers each week for a month to let the surrounding community know we were launching a new church in town.

I could feel the momentum growing, and I was excited!

And although I didn't see the same momentum in my personal fundraising, I didn't stress too much because I had the safety net of the planting group and the sending church. I was too focused on getting this new church up and off the ground.

We opened our doors October 1, 2006. That first Sunday, 268 people showed up! I was blown away!

The next Sunday, we grew by two — 270 people!

On the third Sunday, we almost hit 290! We were not only maintaining attendance numbers, but we were growing. We were an instant church!

Our enthusiastic staff and volunteers worked hard to set up and tear down each week. It was exhausting but extremely rewarding. We were off to an incredible start.

After our third Sunday service, as we packed up the church equipment, my best friend, Ben Kendrew, pulled up. We were headed to the Steelers game — those tickets are hard to come by — and I was thrilled. I couldn't wait to cheer on the Black and Gold and blow off some stress of planting a new church.

As Ben and I drove off, the assistant pastor climbed into the truck that was towing the trailer with all our portable church equipment. His wife was with him.

Ben and I were ten minutes down the road when my cell phone rang.

The assistant pastor's voice was shaking. He'd just been in a wreck. He and his wife were fine, but the truck and the equipment looked bad.

I immediately knew that I had to go to the crash site to be with him and figure out what to do. I gave my ticket back to Ben and started walking back toward the accident.

When I arrived, traffic was backed up for miles going into the city — the truck and portable equipment trailer were blocking both lanes. Steelers fans were not happy!

Now I don't know if my cell phone was on vibrate or if I was in a dead zone, but I didn't get any calls as I walked back to the crash site. As I waited for the assistant pastor and his wife to finish speaking with police, I looked down at my phone and noticed I had a voicemail.

I listened. It was my lead pastor—and he was heated. He was yelling, angry that I'd gone to the Steelers game instead of being with the assistant pastor at the crash site.

In the middle of hearing his voicemail, my phone rang. I answered and he immediately started yelling again, unaware I was already back at the scene. It wasn't his best moment, and I wasn't proud of my reaction either. We were both stressed and upset.

That crash was the beginning of the end.

In the weeks that followed, a decision was made that I was no longer fit to lead the campus. At the turn of the new year, the lead pastor stepped in and began to lead the campus. A few weeks later, I was demoted to be a traveling teaching pastor for the campuses of the multi-site church. My salary immediately decreased by $10,000 and the "safety net" was no longer available. I was paid by what I raised.

A few weeks later, the movie theater informed us that they would be closing for a short season for renovations.

I was dumbfounded.

Here I was again in a financial mess with a wife, two daughters, and a new mortgage. I was being demoted and struggling to raise my salary, which had just been severely cut!

One day, I fell apart in my kitchen. I collapsed under the stress of it all and curled up into the fetal position and lost control of myself. I sobbed. I couldn't breathe. I thought I was having a heart attack. My chest and my head felt like they were going to explode. I had never had an anxiety attack, but I think I had one that day.

Erica crawled down onto the floor with me and held me tightly as I bawled my eyes out.

What had I done? What was I going to do now?

That "Week 3 Crash" and all that followed led to my own crash. I was a wreck. Familiar feelings came rushing back: I felt like a failure... as a husband, as a father, as a pastor.

I didn't know what to do.

I called Randy. I called Dave. I told Ben. They listened to me. They prayed with me. They all advised me to develop a swift exit strategy.

In the end, I was given an ultimatum, but based on the option presented, Erica and I decided to leave immediately — without the opportunity to say goodbye to anyone.

We were kicked out of that nest. And we took a couple of needles to the heart in the process.

Our wings were broken, and we were falling hard with no landing place in sight.

A few weeks later, the new church campus ceased to exist. I was to blame.

A MORE COMFORTABLE NEST

For the first time in my adult life, I was unemployed. I didn't have a job. Erica worked part-time, and she could switch to full-time if necessary, but we had two toddlers. I was scrambling.

I was also hurting. I thought about leaving ministry altogether. I seriously explored becoming a full-time bread delivery truck driver.

Once I knew we were going down, I called the one person I knew who had a pulse on Pittsburgh ministry positions. Brad Henderson was president of the Pittsburgh Kids Foundation, formerly known as the Pittsburgh Youth Network. He was also the chaplain of the Pirates (MLB) and Penguins (NHL). If anyone knew about any ministry jobs, it was Brad.

He made some calls and within a few days, I had three interviews lined up. One was at a great church with two pastor friends I really respected, but I discovered that the position wasn't the right fit. Another was with a newer church looking for a worship director and young adult pastor. I really liked the role but didn't have any relationships there. The other interview was with North Way Christian Community.

It turned out that North Way had changed its vision since I'd last met with Jay.

They were no longer going to build that massive sanctuary—they were going multi-site! North Way had just launched their first campus in Oakland (a university and medical community), and they were looking to plant more. I was interviewed to lead a new worship experience at the original campus and work with young adults with the potential to plant a new campus someday.

I was offered the job. I made sure I didn't have to raise my salary this time, and joined the staff of North Way in May 2007.

We loved the people of North Way. We felt safe. We settled in. We didn't have to move because the commute wasn't that bad. We started to feel comfortable.

Erica and I felt led to try for another baby. I felt secure enough with our combined salaries that we could support another.

Soon we were able to share the news with our family and friends that we were having another baby girl!

That made three daughters!

It was a wonderful summer. Our girls attended Kids GiG at North Way and had a blast. I was working to build the core team and staff of the new worship venue (like a church within a church). I loved my new role.

Everything was going great...

...Until we got the news that Erica's dad had leukemia. We rallied. We prayed. We believed God would heal him. Erica's dad died on September 24, 2007.

Pregnant with our third daughter, Erica had to bury her dad.

On the heels of this tragedy—six days later—I had to launch the new worship service. Erica and I were in no shape to lead anything. It was beyond brutal.

Yet in the midst of tragedy, we experienced the beauty of the church. The people of North Way rallied around us with servant-hearted love. They brought us meals so we didn't have to think about cooking. They even hired a cleaning service for our home. Church leadership and the congregation alike served us while we were recovering from grief on multiple levels.

They instantly became our family and we knew we were home. We were desperate to heal up and put down roots.

 **Key Takeaways**

- Not every good opportunity is a God opportunity.
- Spiritual disciplines (fasting, praying, reading Scripture, etc.) draw us closer to God and help us recognize His voice. (James 4:8)
- Get to know the senior leader(ship) before you accept a position. Interview them as much as they interview you.
- God will allow you to be broken to ensure you lead with humility and dependence on Him. You can choose to humble yourself before the Lord, or He will choose to humble you. (1 Peter 5:6)
- The Church is a community of people who (should) take care of one another, especially in times of trials and tragedy. (Acts 2:42-47)

Application Questions

1. Who are the mentors you have invited to speak into your life?
2. Have you ever had a moment where you knew something shifted in you where God was about to do something new? Try to describe it.
3. Have you ever had a season where you knew God was calling you to do something, but it failed? Describe it.
4. When have you experienced the church serving you in a trying time? How did people show their support?

CHAPTER 4

There's Gotta Be Another Way

I loved serving as a pastor of North Way Christian Community. My family thrived while being a part of this church. I watched Erica and my daughters grow in their relationship with God and others. I grew in my leadership, and I was asked to become the campus pastor of the original campus. That was a tremendous stretch for me, and I nervously welcomed the challenge of leading this large church and staff.

Life and ministry were good!

I was ten years in as a pastor there when I felt God's familiar nudge. I could sense a new opportunity was on the horizon. My role hadn't changed, and neither had my responsibilities, but I started feel something in my gut.

I like to call it my "knower."

And in my knower, I sensed that God was up to something. But to be honest, I was afraid of what that meant for my family and me.

I hesitated to pursue it because I was comfortable. I had a great position and a steady paycheck, and I didn't want to risk losing that.

What about you?

I wonder if you're reading this and you've been feeling the same way. You can sense that God is up to something new in your life, but comfort and familiarity are holding you back.

Maybe you have a new idea that could change the business, but you're hesitant to pitch the idea to the owners because you have a good position.

Maybe you know you're supposed to move to a new city or state, but you have a steady job and a consistent paycheck. It doesn't make sense for you to give all that up for a dream, so you're staying put.

Maybe you've been dating her for years now and you know you want to be with her, but you're scared to "pop the question" and really commit because the relationship is comfortable.

Maybe you've been tiptoeing around the idea of surrendering your life to Jesus. You feel drawn in, but you're uncertain about how your friends might respond. You don't want to stand out in a way that feels uncomfortable or strains the relationships you care about.

Maybe you know it's time for you to go public with your faith in Jesus and leverage the platform that God has given you, but you're worried about the reaction and fallout and not ready to take the risk.

I get it. Believe me. Been there — done that. But…

I firmly believe there are going to be moments in our lives when God messes us up on the inside until we step into what He is calling us to.

However…

I must warn you: some of us step too soon! This is where we get in trouble.

You've read in the previous chapters that I'm writing from experience here.

We move into the new before God tells us to move. We experience internal frustration and get antsy in the waiting, so we grab on to the first opportunity that comes along.

The new position. The new house. The next person who applies for the job. We have to be careful here. We can get ahead of God and grab onto the wrong position. We can get into a house that He hasn't lined up for us. We can hire the wrong person and have to fire them and start the whole process over again.

I have learned from past failures and great insight from mentors in my life that…

God's timing is just as important as His direction.

WAITING SEASON(S)

I learned my lesson with the failed church plant, so I was determined to wait on God's timing. I chose not to seek any opportunities while I continued to serve in my role.

In the Fall of 2017, I was about two years into the frustration of waiting on God's timing when the San Francisco 49ers traded a tight end to the Pittsburgh Steelers: Vance McDonald. After the season ended, he and his family attended a service at North Way. Vance came up to me after the service and asked if we could grab coffee and have a conversation.

We talked for a few hours at a local coffee shop. It was there he told me that the Steelers didn't have a team chaplain.

When he said that, my knower stirred—just a quiet "hmm." I found myself wondering what an NFL chaplain actually does. An Army chaplain made sense. A hospital chaplain I could picture. But what does an NFL chaplain do?

I didn't ask but my interest was piqued.

Vance and I grabbed coffee several times in that off-season, getting to know each other.

Throughout the following Steelers season, we all watched "Big Ben" Roethlisberger and Vance connect on plenty of touchdowns. And if you're a Steelers fan, you might remember the famous Vanimal stiff-arm — the one that went viral on every sports network.

Vance McDonald stiff-arming Chris Conte on September 23, 2018, earning him the nickname, Vanimal. © Cal Sport Media/Alamy Stock Photo

Big Ben hit Vance in the flat. He caught the football, turned up the field, and was immediately met by a Tampa Bay Buccaneers defender (Chris Conte). Vance planted a vicious stiff arm on him and leveled him into the ground. The Steelers sideline and the crowd went wild as Vance ran seventy-five yards into the end zone for the touchdown!

Steelers Nation went crazy! For some reason, I didn't.

As a lifelong Steelers fan, I should've been celebrating, but something happened within me that day. I thought about Vance's wife, Kendi. I wondered if she was there watching him play. I thought about their baby boy. Was Kendi celebrating the touchdown while holding him in her arms?

God's nudge had made me think about Vance from a completely different perspective. Yes, Vance was a Steelers tight end who just scored, but he was first a young husband and father. He wasn't just a professional athlete there for our entertainment. He was a real person.

Funny how the NFL shield can do that. Sometimes seeing these players up on our screens blinds us from seeing they're only human.

God was shifting my heart. I could feel it.

TIME TO JUMP?

When the 2018 season ended, Vance asked if I would lead him and a few other guys in a discipleship group. During that journey, Vance often talked about how he longed for that kind of biblical community in the Steelers locker room, but without a chaplain, it simply wasn't there. And each time mentioned it, something stirred deep within my knower — steady and impossible to ignore.

The needles in my nest were making me uncomfortable again. After three years (THREE YEARS!) of waiting on God to open a door, I began to wonder if that was the "new thing" He was calling me to do.

I questioned my motives. Was it just to get close to these Steelers players? Was it to be famous adjacent? Was it so I could say I was on staff with the Steelers?

I couldn't stop talking about it with Erica, but I would never bring it up to Vance. Was he dropping hints to me as a prayer request? Was he sharing this with our discipleship group because he thought I could be the chaplain?

Then came the day when Vance asked me directly: "Do you know of anyone who would be interested in the chaplain position?"

I finally got up the courage to ask him if he thought I could do it.

He said, "I didn't think you'd be interested, but I'd love to introduce you to Coach Tomlin."

Are you kidding me?

Mike Tomlin is one of the most respected head coaches in the NFL. He's one of the most influential leaders in Pittsburgh and beyond. To be able to sit down for a conversation with him would be a gift, let alone be introduced to him regarding this chaplain role.

Either way, this was going to be awesome!

BEFORE I JUMP...

I knew I needed to tell Scott that this was a possibility. I didn't want to keep any secrets from him. I had learned the hard lessons when I left my first youth pastor position.

I thought it was important to involve him in the process, not just as my boss but also my mentor, I trusted him to shoot straight with me, and I knew he had my (and my family's) best interest at heart. He walked with us through so much, and he knew that I was unsettled and wrestling in my current position.

Scott gave me his blessing to explore the chaplain position.

TIME TO JUMP!

Tomlin, Vance, and I had a great conversation over lunch at the Steelers facility. Tomlin was vetting me. He asked me about my life, marriage, ministry, and family, but said little about the position. We simply got to know each other.

Tomlin ended the meeting by inviting me to attend Organized Team Activities (OTAs) and to speak at mandatory Mini Camp Chapel. OTAs are voluntary team practices held in the late spring, allowing players and coaches their first on-field work, focusing on conditioning, playbook installation, and team chemistry without live tackling or full contact. Mandatory Mini Camp, held in mid-June, is where all the players are required to attend three days of practice, where coaches assess talent, mental processing, and physical readiness, giving young players valuable reps they might not get later.

As a Pittsburgh kid, I was ecstatic!

Over the next five weeks, I saw the ins and outs of the Steelers organization. I toured the Steelers practice facility, saw all six Super Bowl trophies in their display cases, and viewed all the team pictures since 1933. Because of my friendship with Vance, I sat in on the tight end meeting. I stood on the sidelines and interacted with players, coaches, and staff.

It was an incredible experience!

Then came the opportunity to speak at chapel. My heart raced as coaches, players, and staff filed into the team meeting room. Nerves fluttered through me, but I offered what I had. I shared a twenty-minute message about Jesus standing with us in the storms of life and then I closed in prayer.

When I left the facility on the southside, Tomlin said he'd be in touch.

A day went by... nothing. A few days went by... nothing. A week went by... still nothing.

Ten days went by... I still hadn't heard a thing.

At that point I began to think I blew it. I apparently was not the guy, so I settled back into frustration and confusion.

Have you ever been there?

Have you ever stepped out in faith, but there's that wait before you land? It's like getting to the edge of the high dive, and your knees are shaking. All you can see is the water twenty feet below. You eventually get up the nerve to jump, but before you hit the water, you start to question your decision-making skills.

Why did I do this?

These are the mid-jump moments when the enemy of our soul, the devil, provokes us. He messes with our heads mid-leap. He messes with our hearts mid-step. When you take that shot. When you make that move. When you make that sales pitch.

You jump! But then you have to wait—and it can wreak havoc on your soul.

It's in that waiting that we have a choice. Which voice are we going to listen to in that moment? The voice of Truth, the voice of God, who reminds us we're loved and enough no matter what happens? Or the voice of the enemy who whispers the lies…

You're not good enough to get that position. You're obviously not wanted here.

You're crazy to believe YOU could ever do something like this.

If God was really good to you, He wouldn't put you through this.

The confusion I felt mounted to a boiling point. Three years had passed since I felt that first nudge in my knower, and I still hadn't heard back from Tomlin.

I was mad. I was disappointed. I felt like a failure. I wondered if I made things awkward at church. I was embarrassed.

In a gut-wrenching prayer, I asked, "God, what are you doing? C'mon, God! Please!"

C'mon God!

Have you ever prayed that kind of prayer?

"C'mon, God! Where are you? Why are you not coming through?"

"I've been out of work for months! God, where are you? Please provide a job."

"My brother is sick and lying in a hospital bed. C'mon, God! Please heal him.

God, we can't get pregnant! C'mon, God! Why won't you do this for us?"

"God, this world is going crazy! Where are you? Step in and fix this. C'mon, God!"

We've all had a "C'mon God" moment in some shape or form.

While I was having my "C'mon God" meltdown and waiting to hear back from Tomlin, I was still the pastor of North Way's Wexford Campus.

We were beginning a new discipleship experience, and I traveled to a church on the West Coast for some training. During one of the sessions, the facilitators sent us out for what they called a guided prayer experience.

One trainer said, "Just follow the prayer guide. Read the Scriptures on the page and then write out your prayers after each passage."

At the very top of the page was Isaiah 43:18–19. I opened my Bible and read, "Forget the former things; do not dwell on the past. See, I am doing a new thing! Now it springs up; do you not perceive it? I am making a way in the wilderness and streams in the wasteland."

I remember feeling frustrated and even disappointed. I knew God was doing something new in my life, I just couldn't perceive it!

The facilitators instructed us to write our prayers, so here's exactly what I wrote in my journal.

"God, I'm trying to discern the new that You are doing in my life. Is it at North Way? Is it with the Steelers? Is it with both of them? Is it something else completely different?

Either way, God, I need clarity, so I lay all of this down at Your feet because I'm anxious to know what You want for me, my family, and my church family. You may have something else entirely in mind, but I can sense that You have been up to something new for a long time in my life."

I put the pen down in frustration.

The next passage to read and journal from was Ezekiel 37:1–14.

> "The hand of the Lord was on me, and he brought me out by the Spirit of the Lord and set me in the middle of a valley; it was full of bones. He led me back and forth among them, and I saw a great many bones on the floor of the valley, bones that were very dry. He asked me, "Son of man, can these bones live?"
>
> I said, "Sovereign Lord, you alone know."
>
> Then he said to me, "Prophesy to these bones and say to them, 'Dry bones, hear the word of the Lord! This is what the Sovereign Lord

says to these bones: I will make breath enter you, and you will come to life. I will attach tendons to you and make flesh come upon you and cover you with skin; I will put breath in you, and you will come to life. Then you will know that I am the Lord.'"

So I prophesied as I was commanded. And as I was prophesying, there was a noise, a rattling sound, and the bones came together, bone to bone. I looked, and tendons and flesh appeared on them and skin covered them, but there was no breath in them.

Then he said to me, "Prophesy to the breath; prophesy, son of man, and say to it, 'This is what the Sovereign Lord says: Come, breath, from the four winds and breathe into these slain, that they may live.'" So I prophesied as he commanded me, and breath entered them; they came to life and stood up on their feet—a vast army.

Then he said to me: "Son of man, these bones are the people of Israel. They say, 'Our bones are dried up and our hope is gone; we are cut off.' Therefore prophesy and say to them: 'This is what the Sovereign Lord says: My people, I am going to open your graves and bring you up from them; I will bring you back to the land of Israel. Then you, my people, will know that I am the Lord, when I open your graves and bring you up from them. I will put my Spirit in you and you will live, and I will settle you in your own land. Then you will know that I the Lord have spoken, and I have done it, declares the Lord.'"

God downloaded this vision to Ezekiel with a powerful lesson for real life. Here's the lesson as I saw it.

God said, "Ezekiel, I want you to say exactly what I tell you to say," and Ezekiel said it.

Boom! A supernatural move of God took take place. Again... "Ezekiel... Do exactly what I tell you to do." Ezekiel did it. Boom! Another supernatural move.

God revealed to Ezekiel that if and when He obeyed, God would move powerfully in his life and restore the people of Israel back into a relationship with God.

The last sentence of this passage hit me in my chest. "Then you will know that I, the Lord, have spoken, and I have done what I said. Yes, the Lord has spoken!" (Ezek. 37:14 [NIV])

I picked up my pen and started writing, "*God, speak. Your servant is listening.*"

I closed my eyes to focus in and listened for His voice, and… I heard God speak!

When I say that I heard God speak, you might think I'm strange. And I understand. Growing up, whenever someone claimed they'd heard God, I quietly wrote them off as odd.

Let me try to explain what I mean.

I've never heard the audible voice of God, booming from the heavens exclaiming, "Thus sayeth the Lord to Kent Chevalier!" It wasn't like that at all.

Instead, after reading Ezekiel 37:14, a phrase jumped into my heart and mind. In my knower, I felt God say…

"Kent, just settle down. Do what I say to do when I tell you to do it. Nothing more, nothing less. That way you know it's me."

It was an impression. It was a clear command. It was evident that God was speaking to me through this Ezekiel passage, encouraging me to be obedient.

The main way God speaks to us is through His Word, the Bible. The more we read it, meditate on it, and pray through it, the clearer His voice and direction becomes in our lives. The Holy Spirit will never reveal anything that is contrary to God's revealed Word.

So, with my heart beating fast and a warmth in my chest, I quickly wrote that word from the Lord in my journal. At that very moment, I felt certain something was about to break into my three-year wait. I wrote these words as a prayer.

"I have a great thing going with North Way, God. I'm just wondering what you're doing with the Steelers' chaplain role. Am I initiating that? If so, I lay it down, and I will wait for you."

That question that I asked God was crucial! Am I initiating?

My mentor, Dave Buehring, taught me a powerful lesson about initiating things ahead of God's direction and timing. He said, "What God initiates, He permeates. What we initiate, we have to sustain."

What we start, we have to sustain in our own strength. Our own power. Our own provision.

Our own ideas.

What God initiates, He permeates with his presence, power, and provision. God's ideas are much better than mine, and I wanted what God wanted, so I laid it all down.

It was a powerful moment for me!

TIMELY TEXT

My thoughts were interrupted as I heard the facilitators over the loud speaker: "The prayer experience is over. Please make your way back to the room." I gathered up my Bible and prayer journal. As I stood up to leave, Tomlin texted me, "Can you grab lunch in the next few days to talk about the position?"

Are you kidding me? This was minutes after I had laid the chaplain position down! Was God now opening the door that I thought was closed, in His timing?

My hands trembled as I called Erica. I said, "I think I'm about to become the chaplain of the Pittsburgh Steelers!" Mind you, I hadn't even been offered the position, but I just knew something was about to break through.

When I got back from California, I went to lunch with Tomlin.

He started out by offering me the position, and went on to cast his vision for the chaplain role.

He said, "I'm looking for a local Pittsburgh couple who can pastor this team."

Wait! What? You want my wife to do this too? I'd get to work with my wife? Awesome!

He continued, "I want a guy who can lead Bible studies for the players and coaches. I want him to speak and lead chapels before the games. I'm looking for his wife to lead Bible studies for the coaches' wives and players' wives or girlfriends. I want this couple to come alongside the couples on this team."

I loved everything I was hearing, but then he said...

"This position is not hired by the Steelers. I would like for you to consider joining the staff of Athletes in Action."

My heart dropped. Tomlin continued talking, but I stopped listening.

It was like he punched me in my teeth. I knew exactly what this meant.

I was familiar with Athletes in Action, a sports ministry of the missions organization, Cru (formerly known as Campus Crusade for Christ).

I knew that people with AIA have to raise their full-time salaries, benefits, and ministry budgets.

As Tomlin spoke, I began to shut down the opportunity in my mind. In fact, I don't remember anything else he said beyond that point because I was having a conversation with God.

God, you're kidding me! I have three teenage daughters! God, I'm staring three college tuitions right in the face! God, I have to pay for three weddings!

There's no way you want me to step away from a secure income and a great position to become a full-time missionary!

There's gotta be another way!

IN GOD WE TRUST?

I am amazed at how quickly my "IOU" fear reared its ugly head. My internal reaction to Tomlin's job offer revealed where I placed my trust.

My trust was not fully in the God I've been preaching for twenty-eight years. My trust was in a consistent paycheck. My trust was in a comfortable position. My trust was in me providing for my family.

Whenever I tell this part of the story, I get embarrassed. I'm supposed to be this faith-filled pastor who doesn't struggle with this kind of thing. Truth be told, I do.

Do you?

I'm wondering if you can relate.

I don't think I'm alone in this. I think we all struggle to trust God fully.

I snapped back to the conversation. I agreed to speak with the leadership of AIA and continue the process. I was cordial and said all the right words, but internally, I was pulling the plug.

Bottom line... I was afraid. I was afraid to jump again.

The last few times I made the leap, it hurt my family and me. It put us in financial stress. We were finally in a good place — comfortable.

I went home to tell Erica. She wasn't thrilled at the idea of raising our salary again. In our minds, we had called it quits, but we didn't shut down the process because I had given Tomlin my word.

We agreed to fast and pray. We agreed to see it through.

💡 Key Takeaways

- God's timing is just as important as His direction.
- God is seldom early, but He is never late.
- The enemy's voice accuses and condemns. God's voice convicts and encourages.
- The main way God speaks is through the Bible.
- "What God initiates, He permeates. What we initiate, we have to sustain."

❓ Application Questions

1. When have you rushed ahead of God's timing? How did it impact your life?
2. What have been your "C'mon, God!" moments and prayers? How did God answer?
3. Have you ever heard God's voice? Describe your experience.
4. Do you have a regular rhythm of reading God's word? What is it?
5. Have you ever initiated something that God never intended for you? How did that affect you?

CHAPTER 5

Lessons from a Nest

I was in my chair in the early morning. It's my spot to read my Bible and spend time in prayer with the Lord. Because it was late June in Pittsburgh, Erica was outside on our back patio doing the same. Our three teenage daughters were still sleeping when I suddenly heard Erica scream my name.

I ran outside to discover her frozen in fear. She pointed to the fern beside her. It was moving. Something was in there — possibly a snake — and she was only feet from it.

I wandered into the yard and picked up a stick — my makeshift weapon of choice. I'm afraid of snakes. I don't like them one bit. But in that moment, "manning up" apparently meant arming myself with a twig.

I moved toward the fern, inch by inch. I slipped the stick into the leaves and in an instant a bird flew out! I jumped back, startled — but flooded with relief it wasn't a snake.

Peering inside, I saw a nest holding three eggs. Over the next several weeks, when Erica and I went out on the patio to pray and read Scripture, we would peek in on the eggs. One day, they hatched. We could hear the tiny birds chirping as mommy bird swooped down to feed them while dad perched himself on our string lights to keep an eye out. If we wandered too close, he'd scold us with sharp chirps.

As we actively waited — fasting, praying, reading Scripture, and seeking wise counsel — on the chaplain opportunity, the words of Jesus came to both of our minds. Recorded in Matthew 6:26 (NIV) is Jesus' reminder: "Look at the birds of the air. They do not sow or reap or store away in barns, and yet your Heavenly Father feeds them. Are you not much more valuable than they?" Talk about the Scriptures coming alive! These birds on our back patio were a living illustration of God's provision unfolding right before our eyes.

As we walked through the process, God schooled us on what we really trusted in this life. He began to shift our hearts to practice what we'd been preaching all these years. To follow Jesus, no matter what the cost. To obey God even when you can't see the end from the beginning. To trust in the principle that my dad taught me: "When God guides, He always provides."

We calculated the risk involved. Raising two full-time salaries, benefits, and a ministry budget wasn't a small jump. It required a huge leap of faith to leave our current jobs that provided consistent paychecks every two weeks.

But we couldn't deny that God was calling us to join the staff of AIA. He wasn't asking — He was telling us, in prayer and through the Scriptures and wise mentors. We realized that we would've been disobedient to God if we didn't follow His lead.

We told our three daughters about the opportunity and asked what they thought. We explained that we'd been fasting and praying about the decision. They were excited about it and relieved to know that they wouldn't have to move away from home or their school.

We weighed it all. We counted the cost.

In unity, Erica and I took the step in our hearts as fear fought with our faith. We embraced the fear of the unknown to jump into our God-given purpose.

Together, we agreed that we would do it even though we were afraid.

But we didn't tell anyone. Not yet.

We knew *when* we needed to communicate our decision to Tomlin and the leadership of AIA. However, we waited because we wanted to give God a runway to land on to reveal anything we had missed. We gave the Holy Spirit an opportunity to breathe on what we were convinced God was calling us to do. We'll talk more about the value of the "Prayer Runway" in Chapter 12.

We waited a few days for God to confirm our decision.

―――

I think this is an important place to stop and ask you some questions.

How are you making life-altering decisions? A job change. A move. College. Marriage. Do you have a God-honoring process by which you make big decisions?

Are you just doing whatever feels best, or are you calculating the risk? Are you asking God and godly mentors who will point you to Truth?

If you're married, are you involving your spouse, or are you running ahead and making the decision on your own?

If you have kids, how are you involving them in the decision?

Within days of communicating our decision—first to our daughters, then to our small circle of trust, then to Tomlin and the AIA leadership—we boarded a plane to Fort Collins, Colorado to sign on the dotted line and become full-time missionaries. This happened to coincide with Cru's national conference where more than 5,000 state-side missionaries gathered at Colorado State University for worship, teaching, and training.

We signed the papers! We did it!

We stepped out, but to be honest we were still freaking out. Even though we knew that God was calling us to do this, fear and anxiousness were getting the best of us.

We met the leadership of AIA face to face for the first time. They held meetings to get us up to speed since we would be starting with the Steelers right away. It was a whirlwind—overwhelming, to say the least.

Reality was setting in fast: the huge weight of this decision, the enormous amount of money we would have to raise each year! We were learning things we had no category for at that time. It was exhilarating and stressful all at once.

That night, we were exhausted and couldn't wait to close our eyes and drift off to sleep.

I'm quicker than Erica with my nighttime routine, so I was already in bed when I heard her crying in the hotel bathroom. All the stress and emotions of this decision had finally caught up with her. If she were writing this, she'd tell you she was confident in God, yet at the same time nervous—scared and stressed, even while knowing God's direction was clear.

She tossed and turned all night and woke up before dawn for a run—her sanctuary of rhythm and prayer. With worship music in her ears, she poured her heart out to God, and somewhere along the quiet streets, tears began to fall.

In the middle of that unfamiliar city, she had a desperate "C'mon, God!" moment. Through sobs, she cried out, "God, I know You're calling us to do this, but I need a confirmation I can hold onto that You are definitely in this."

She had no idea what was about to happen.

Key Takeaways

- Faith is not an absence of fear. Faith is trusting God amidst your fears.
- When God guides, He always provides.
- There will always be a cost to obeying God's call on your life.
- When it comes to your calling, God does not ask. He tells.
- "What God reveals is not meant to be negotiated. It's meant to be obeyed." — Dave Buehring

Application Questions

1. Have you ever had a moment when the Bible came alive and the words jumped off the page and into your heart? Describe it...
2. What is your God-honoring process for making decisions?
3. Is your "yes" to God louder than your fear?
4. What is your way of handling stress?
5. Have you ever had a breakdown with God where you cried out to Him?

CHAPTER 6

When God Shows Up and Shows Off!

I woke up, and Erica wasn't in bed. I didn't know she had gone for a run. The night had been rough; stress had stolen our sleep. I felt it, the whispering doubts about the leap we had just taken.

We had jumped, plunging headfirst into the unknown. But my mind screamed …Whyyyyy did I dooooo this?

Erica returned from her run, her eyes wet and her voice trembling as she told me that she had broken down and cried out to the Lord. I did my best to console her, but I knew only God could soothe the storm inside.

We got ready and headed to the main session at Cru19. Thousands of Cru missionaries had gathered in Colorado State University's basketball coliseum. At center court sat a round stage with a Jumbotron suspended above it. We chose seats on the floor, a few rows back from the stage.

The music began, and more than 5,000 missionaries lifted their voices in worship.

On the far side of the stage, we noticed a painter at work. We couldn't see what he was creating—only the back of the canvas—and the cameras intentionally kept his art off the Jumbotron. As we sang, the painter moved furiously. The arena was buzzing with curiosity.

As the final song neared its end, the painter stepped back from his creation, and the camera finally focused in. The music reached a crescendo and everyone looked at the Jumbotron...

What do you think the painter painted that morning?

Brian Peterson's painting at Cru19.

Erica and I looked at each other and we both began to cry! The painting of baby birds in a nest was God's incredibly specific word to her. He heard her desperate prayer early that morning and answered in confirmation with His precise fashion.

The detail of this painting is spectacular! Baby birds in a nest, crying out—completely dependent, fully ready to receive. Clusters of grapes, still attached to the vine, being fed to them.

I can't fully capture the weight of that moment for Erica and me. And just when we thought it couldn't get any more incredible, the next part hit us—even wilder than we could've imagined.

It seemed that everyone in Cru knew who the painter, Brian Peterson, was—except for us.

In 2015, Brian became a devoted Christian, which ultimately reignited his passion for creativity and his desire to create alongside God. For the first time in his life, Brian connected his love for art, his community, and Jesus to form Faces of Mankind, a non-profit organization focused on homelessness and the rehabilitation of our neighbors. Faces of Mankind has expanded to many cities across the nation, with Faces of Santa Ana, California, being the first.

Everybody in the basketball arena was expecting Brian to paint a face—the face of Jesus, the face of a disciple, somebody's face! That was what he and his ministry were known for. When the emcee brought him up on the platform for an interview, he also introduced a precious lady Brian met through Faces of Santa Ana.

Then the question on everyone's mind came: "Why didn't you paint a face?"

His answer floored Erica and me. "It was the weirdest thing, Brian said. "I had a plan of what I wanted to paint coming into today, but when I woke up this morning, I felt like God was telling me to paint birds in a nest."

Are you kidding me?

(I'm crying my eyes out as I write this testimony for you.)

Did God wake this guy up that morning and plant birds on his mind and heart just to give Erica and me the courage we needed to keep going?

I left the session that day ready to run through a brick wall. God showed up and showed off for us. He knew Erica and I needed this confirmation.

Even though we were still afraid of the unknown, we left that day confident that God was going to take care of us every step of the way.

A week later, I reported to the Steelers training camp at St. Vincent College in Latrobe, Pennsylvania. There was no turning back now!

💡 Key Takeaways

- God hears every cry of your heart. He knows exactly what you need at the right time.
- Human relationships cannot fix or console the deepest cries of our heart. Only God can.
- God can use anything or anybody to speak to you.
- Whenever you feel afraid or your faith is lacking, hold on to the divine altar points where God showed up and showed off.
- Place your confidence for the future in God's past, present, and future promises.

❓ Application Questions

1. Has God ever astounded you with the way He answered your cry? Describe it.
2. Where do you struggle to place your confidence in God's promises?
3. Do you have a "Look at what God has done!" story you need to share with people? Are you sharing it? If not, why?

CHAPTER 7

Do It Afraid

"This is my story. This is my song. Praising my Savior all the day long."

These lyrics from the Fanny Crosby hymn "Blessed Assurance" are imprinted on my soul. I cannot sing that song without thinking of my Grandma Chevalier. She was my family's matriarch of faith—a tough yet tender woman who raised eleven children in the ways, character, and mission of Jesus.

When I sing "Blessed Assurance," I'm flooded with gratefulness that salvation through Jesus Christ is my story. When I sing it, I picture my Grandma Chevy, my dad and his siblings, and my cousins at Hollow Rock Camp in Toronto, Ohio. I grew up going to this family camp every summer. I can picture them worshiping God by singing this old hymn in the open-air tabernacle. When I do, tears come, because I'm grateful for the legacy of faith in my family.

The book you are holding is woven into my faith story.

I want my story to point to Jesus' story.

I want it to point to God's call on your life. I believe God wanted me to write this story to testify about what God has done in Erica's life and mine. My hope is that it unleashes the courage in you to embrace the fear of the unknown and step boldly into your God-given purpose.

It's been seven years since Erica and I jumped. We're trusting God for everything as full-time missionaries, and it's still scary at times, but it's been amazing to watch God do His thing. He's delivered on His promises in ways we did not expect. He's blown our minds with His provision. Our faith has been (and is being) stretched in ways we didn't know it needed to be stretched. Our faith has been (and continues to be) brought alive in ways we didn't know our faith was dead. Time and time again, God has shown himself faithful.

"Look at what God has done!"

This has become a mantra for Erica and me along this faith-stretching journey. Time and again, we've stood back and said, "Look at what God has done!" My hope is that you experience similar moments of awe and growth in your faith. I want you to live a faith that moves you to step out in obedience to do the hard things, and to jump boldly with us.

DO IT AFRAID DAILY

Living by faith isn't a single, dramatic jump—it's a daily choice to surrender in both the big moments and the small ones. It means trusting God to lead us through life's uncertainties. Erica and I stepped into the unknown world of the NFL, and that leap opened the door to experiences that have been both exhilarating and challenging.

That initial leap was followed by countless smaller ones, each requiring courage and trust. Through it all, God had already been preparing us for the daily challenges and opportunities that lay ahead.

Something awful happened ten days into my first Steelers training camp—a coach tragically died in his sleep. Tomlin called me down to his room and asked me to address the men after he began the team meeting. I had never spoken to the entire team and all the coaches in any setting, and now I was assigned to give words of comfort and guidance. I had no clue what to say, so I prayed and God gave me a phrase to share with the team. "Counseling is not for the weak. It's for the wise." This led the way for the men to talk openly about their grief. God helped me do it afraid. He had prepared me for that moment.

One night before the Steelers played the Patriots in New England, God prompted me to do something difficult. Up until this point, whenever I gave an invitation for men to follow Jesus Christ, I would ask privately — with every head bowed and eyes closed. But that night, God challenged me to invite the guys to make a public confession by standing before their teammates and coaches. As three men stepped forward, I felt God urging me to encourage them to take the next step of baptism. God helped me do it afraid, and two men accepted the challenge and were baptized the next morning in the hotel pool.

One of the privileges of walking alongside the men and women of the NFL is being asked to officiate weddings and meet with couples for pre-marital counseling. I've officiated hundreds of weddings over twenty-eight years of ministry, but something shifted in my heart when I realized my words would be heard by hundreds of thousands on social media and written about in popular publications like *People* magazine. There was a temptation to shape my words around public opinion, but God helped Erica and me do it afraid — by faithfully sharing His truth in our pre-marriage counseling sessions and simply being ourselves in those settings.

At one point in this journey, God prompted me to privately call out pastors and Christians I know who post horrible things about players and coaches on social media during or after a performance. God challenged me to help people understand that these men (and their families) are real people and not just entertainers. Every time I must have a conversation, God helps me do it afraid.

Being NFL chaplains comes with some incredible highs and lows. We've had the privilege of leading Bible studies, baby dedication services, baptisms, and weddings. We've also walked closely with people during some of life's hardest moments—team trades, cross-country moves, miscarriage, deaths in the family, and divorces. Each season, we say hello to new players, coaches, and their families, but we also say goodbye. Every new NFL season brings amazing opportunities and difficult challenges.

Erica and I did not feel like we were ready for any of these daily "do it afraid" stories, but God equipped us for every good work that He prepared in advance for us to do.

Look at what God has done.

WILL YOU JUMP?

The danger of writing this book is that you might think Erica and I are something we're not. We're not saints—just ask our daughters. We're ordinary people who have been forever changed by the things of God, no longer satisfied with what this world offers. All Erica and I want is to be obedient to God's call on our lives, and I wanted to write this story to tell you that we almost missed it because fear was driving our decisions.

I almost missed out.

My "IOU"—fear of not having enough—almost killed this call. My past experiences and failures almost derailed God's purpose for my life. God had to work overtime to convince me because I was afraid to embrace the fear of the unknown. I was afraid to jump into my God-given purpose for this season of my life.

I don't want you to miss out.

The reason I share this "Look at what God has done!" story with you is because I wonder: Are you missing out on God's call on your life?

Have you grown too comfortable?

Are you trusting in a consistent paycheck? Are you trusting in a secure position?

Are you trusting in a person instead of God?

You know God's been calling you to step out. But you're hesitant. You're stalling.

You've walked away from that God-sized dream. You've squashed the idea because it seems too risky. Someone told you it doesn't make logical sense.

There might be good reason for not doing it. The question you have to ask yourself is, "Is it a God reason?"

Many of us have something we'd love to accomplish, but there is always an excuse for not doing it. It's a dream in our gut we'd love to turn into a reality. An opportunity within our grasp, but the risk seems too great, and something is holding us back. A God-sized vision but an empty bank account.

What is holding you back? Why won't you jump? What is keeping you on top of the ledge?

Fear.

Knees-knocking, mind-racing, heart-thumping fear.

Fear of failure. Fear of what others might think. Fear of your past catching up with you.

Fear of not providing for your family. Fear of not having enough.

I'll share with you what God spoke to me when I was stressing about financial provision for my family: "You are not your family's provider. I Am. That position is already filled. That doesn't mean you don't work hard, but I am your family's Provider."

That truth was a bolt of correction, and I needed to hear it. I think you need to hear it, too.

Don't let the devil rob you of what God has in store for you. He's not short of cash.

His resources will always follow His call. If He called you to it, He'll provide for it.

You know in your knower that you're supposed to do it.

My testimony is meant to encourage you:

Do it afraid.

Any God-sized dream will involve risk. Do it afraid.

Planting a church is hard. Do it afraid.

Moving your family away is scary. Do it afraid.

It's time to pop the question and commit to her in marriage. Do it afraid.

You know God wants you to pitch that idea to your boss. Do it afraid.

God wants you to share your faith in Jesus with your neighbor. Do it afraid.

You know God is calling you to adopt a child. Do it afraid.

God's calling you to leave your job and go to the mission field. Do it afraid.

It's time for you to go all in on following Jesus today. Do it afraid.

I believe God is raising up men and women in this generation who will step out in bold faith. He is looking for calling-jumpers: those willing to leap, even in the uncertainty of our cultural climate. I believe God is calling His Church to step into new things. He said: "Forget the former things; do not dwell on the past. See, I'm doing a new thing! Now it springs up; do you not perceive it? I am making a way in the wilderness and streams in the wasteland." (Isa. 43:18–19 [NIV])

I don't know the "new" that God is calling you personally to do, but I know God. And I know He is making a way for you. He will provide for you along the journey. His presence will go before you, and His hand will be upon you.

The question I want to leave you with is: Will you follow Jesus' example and do it afraid?

Let me explain.

Jesus saw the brutal path to the cross. He asked God if there was another way.

Luke 22:41–44 records, "And [Jesus] withdrew from them about a stone's throw, and knelt down and prayed, saying, 'Father, if you are willing, remove this cup from me. Nevertheless, not my will, but yours, be done.' And there appeared to him an angel from heaven, strengthening him. And being in agony he prayed more earnestly; and his sweat became like great drops of blood falling down to the ground."

Jesus was in agony. As he prayed, he began to sweat drops of blood. This is a rare medical condition known as Hematidrosis. It's rare, but it is real. Doctors tell us the sweat glands are surrounded by tiny blood vessels that can constrict and then dilate to the point of rupturing, causing blood to fuse into the sweat glands. The cause of this is extreme mental or physical pain.

In the other Gospel accounts, we see the level of Jesus' anguish when he said, "My soul is overwhelmed with sorrow to the point of death." (Matt. 26:38 [NIV])

Jesus was afraid. He was overwhelmed. He was anxious beyond imagination, and He was pleading with God for another way to accomplish His will.

God answered His Son's prayer. He ultimately said "no." God would not remove that cup of wrath. It had to be done to pay for the penalty of my sin and yours.

So, Jesus did it. He willingly submitted to God's call on His life, and knowing the promised joy that lay before Him, Jesus endured the pain of the cross. He died a gruesome death. As an innocent man, he was brutally tortured, crucified, and his body was laid in a borrowed tomb.

And three days later, Jesus rose from that grave! More than 500 eyewitnesses saw Him alive!

Jesus embraced the fear and sting of death, and He conquered it. He overcame!

The resurrection of Jesus Christ changes everything!

I believe that God is calling you to join Jesus by stepping out in that kind of trust and faith, to do it afraid.

You know what "it" is. It stirs deep in your knower. God is calling you to embrace the fear of the unknown.

He wants to use you—to breathe life into a broken heart, to mend a marriage, to introduce someone to Jesus, to uniquely shine in your corner of the world.

But here's the thing...

He won't hand you the full map. He won't reveal every step. He gives you just enough light to take the next one.

Will you let your "yes" roar louder than your fear?

You may not see the whole path yet, but you feel the tug in your heart. That's enough. Take the step. Trust Him. Leap and let God do the rest.

Do it afraid.

Key Takeaways

- God is your (and your family's) Provider. Jehovah Jireh.
- Fear has the potential to kill God's call on your life.
- Once you taste God's extraordinary provision and grace, it will ruin you for the ordinary things this world has to offer.
- Jesus can relate to your fear. He overcame His. So can you.
- You have a faith story that is worth sharing. People need to hear it.

Application Questions

1. What is your legacy of faith in the generations before you? What do you want your legacy of faith to be for generations that follow you?
2. Have you ever considered how your way of providing for your family could actually be hindering you and them from experiencing God as Provider?
3. What are you trusting in that God is calling you to lay down on the altar?
4. What is "it" that you know in your knower God is calling you to do?
5. What has fear killed that you need to resurrect from the grave?

PART 2

L.E.A.P. Before You Jump

PART 2: L.E.A.P. BEFORE YOU JUMP

The second half of this book is going to be the framework that Erica and I learned to make this type of decision. We learned to L.E.A.P. before we jump.

She and I obviously learned the hard way, and I'd rather you learn from our mistakes before you trip, fall, or miss the landing zone like we did. I hope this section of the book will help you avoid some of the pain, but I also think we learn that God speaks loudest when we're falling or have already hit the rocks. Or maybe we're just positioned to listen better when we're in pain because we recognize our overwhelming need for Him.

I want to guide you through a series of practical decisions found in Scripture that we've learned over three decades of following Jesus together. Along the way, great mentors taught us these and now I want to share with you what we did before taking the leap this time.

This L.E.A.P. framework is not a list of action steps. It's harmonious. These aren't steps to follow in exact order, but a collection of action items that are a lifestyle of following Jesus.

L.E.A.P. is more of a life posture than it is a linear process. It's an attitude of the heart. A way of a life that is submitted to the Lordship of Jesus. It is a position of surrender. Palms up. Head bowed. Giving your all and ready to receive all God wants to give you.

This list is not exhaustive by any means, but this eight-part framework has helped Erica and me make life-altering decisions. I hope it helps you as you consider the call to jump into your God-given purpose.

Let God Lead
Express Your Fears
Ask For Wisdom
P.R.A.Y. Through It
  Prayer Runway
  Read God's Word
  Active Waiting
  Yield To God's Call

CHAPTER 8

Let God Lead

*"What God initiates, He permeates.
What you initiate, you have to sustain."*
Dave Buehring

*"The Lord himself goes before you and will be with you;
he will never leave you nor forsake you.
Do not be afraid; do not be discouraged."*
Deuteronomy 31:8

I like to be in the driver's seat. I like to be in control. I feel more relaxed in the driver's seat and struggle when I'm the passenger. Whenever we go somewhere as a family, I usually drive—but when I have to ride shotgun, I tend to tell my wife and daughters how to drive. Erica sticks to the speed limit, and I'm constantly checking the side mirrors and telling her when to switch lanes to pass the slow pokes. When I'm in an Uber, I can't even look out the windows without the urge to tell the driver how to do their job. I'm working on it and improving—but I'd still rather be in control.

What about you? I know I'm not the only one who likes to be in the driver's seat. What about in life? I like to be in control of my life. Don't you?

We think we're in control of our lives. Breaking news. We're not! And we should know that by now.

Proverbs 16:9 (NIV) reminds us "In their hearts humans plan their course, but the Lord establishes their steps."

God is ultimately in control. He is sovereign, meaning He's in charge of it all. He's the Supreme Authority over everything we see and experience.

Carrie Underwood's famous song "Jesus, Take the Wheel" reminds us all that we have a habit of taking the wheel of our lives out of God's sovereign hands. It's only when we get in a jam or we're headed toward a wreck that we see the need to hand life's wheel back over to Him. God establishes the beginning from the end, but if you're like me, you sometimes forget, grab the wheel, and kick Him out of the driver's seat. Or we tell Him He can lead our lives, but keep telling Him how to drive.

Jesus, take the wheel! But I need you to turn here. Pass them. Don't stop there. Switch lanes now. Put the pedal to the metal, Jesus!

When I was a little boy in the passenger seat, I never told my parents how to drive. Why? Three reasons.

First, I trusted my parents to drive me. They knew how to get me where I needed to go, when I needed to get there—details I couldn't even process as a kid.

Second, I didn't know how to drive. My parents had the knowledge and experience I lacked.

Third, I've always been directionally challenged. As a little guy, I had no sense of direction — and I still have no clue where I'm going today. Even if I've "been there" a hundred times, my Maps app is always on, guiding me along the way.

This posture of "Let God Lead" is a plea to return to a child-like faith in Jesus' sovereign ability to drive us and get us where we need to go in life. It's a full weight-bearing trust in Him that He knows the exact time we need to be there. It's a recognition that we don't know how to drive, and if we choose to get behind the wheel, we'll end up crashing and making a wreck of our lives and possibly others.

LET

Let is a word of surrender. It's a conscious choice to give over control, a willingness to step aside. *Let* is a little word with powerful implications. It's a personal decision to lead a selfish heart.

"Follow your heart" is misguided advice. We need to lead our hearts. That's what *let* does. It leads our heart, will, and passions to surrender to the Lordship of Jesus Christ.

Jesus is either Lord of all or He's not Lord at all.

Let leads the heart to submit to the One who created the heart. *Let* takes the emotion out of any decision and willingly allows the Creator to guide the created.

GOD

God is the best driver.

God is all knowing. God is all powerful. God is fully present everywhere and at every moment in time. God was there when you were formed, at the moment of conception. God is with you now, as you read these words, and God is already present at the moment you will take your last breath. You have no idea when or where that will be, yet God is there with you and your future self. He's not bound by our framework of time and space. God is there — past, present, and future — in all of His fullness, beyond anything we can begin to fathom.

When we step back and absorb that reality of God's preeminence, how can we think we know how to better drive our lives? We shouldn't think twice about letting go of the wheel and letting God do whatever He wants, whenever He wants, in our lives. His way will always be better than ours. His direction and timing will always surpass our directionally challenged driving.

Compared to God, you and I have no clue how to drive. God is the best driver. He just is.

He always will be.

LEAD

With that in mind, doesn't it make sense to hand over the keys of leadership to God? To let the Best Driver of your life take the wheel, guiding you along roads you cannot see. It's the wise move.

The sure move. The best thing we can do is follow His lead, trusting His hands on the wheel and His eyes on the road ahead.

There's a captivating story recorded in the pages of Joshua 3 and 4. God was very clear with Joshua: tell the people to follow His presence into the raging river. Joshua's command to the people of Israel was essentially, "God will lead us, and we will follow."

At that time, the Ark of the Covenant served as the physical place of God's presence.

Stop and think about this for one second. Almighty God, unbound by time and space, graced the people of Israel with His presence in a physical place, for their benefit.

Joshua commanded the people to keep their eyes on the Ark and be ready to move as soon as God moved. God was about to lead them over unfamiliar ground. He was about to lead them down a path their generation had never traveled before. It was new territory, so without the Lord's guidance and His leadership, the people wouldn't know which direction to take.

This didn't make logical sense as they waited on God to move. It was hard for the people of Israel to wait for God to move—no wonder it's difficult for us.

Dave Buehring shared that powerful lesson with me. He said, "What God initiates, He permeates. What you initiate, you have to sustain." Stop and read that again.

Many of us step first and then ask God to bless us with his presence. I'm guilty of that. Are you?

"God, here's what I want to do. Will you bless it?"

"God, I have an idea. Will you provide for it?"

"God, I'm going to start this business. Can you get behind it and make it successful?"

If you search the Scriptures, you won't find a single example of God working this way. What you'll find is person after person, leader after leader, choosing to be obedient to God's leadership in their life. The success stories filled with God's blessings are the stories where people do what God tells them to do. They go where God tells them to go.

God leads. His people follow.

We need to become people who follow God's leading. We need to learn from Jesus' example of doing only what He saw the Father doing. Jesus said in John 5:19 (NIV), "Very truly I tell you, the Son can do nothing by himself; he can do only what he sees his Father doing, because whatever the Father does the Son also does."

It would be wise to follow Jesus' example.

Be honest with yourself. When you lead your life, you don't know what you're doing. You don't know where you're going. You don't even have a category for the best way to lead yourself, let alone others. You may think you can drive, but an honest evaluation will show you what a poor driver you are compared to God, the Creator and Sustainer of your life.

The best option is… let God lead.

I know it's scary to hand over the wheel. But God is the best driver. You can trust Him to lead you.

CHAPTER 9

Express Your Fears

*"The presence of fear does not mean you have no faith.
Fear visits everyone. But make your fear a visitor
and not a resident."*
Max Lucado

"Lord, I believe; Help my unbelief."
Mark 9:24

I'll never forget when Mike Tomlin told me the chaplain position was not hired by the Pittsburgh Steelers. When he asked me to consider joining the staff of Athletes in Action, a sports ministry of the global missions organization, Cru, I knew it meant I'd have to raise 100 percent of my salary and even more to take the job.

I was shocked, instantly frustrated, irritated. I tried to hide it. I shifted in my seat. I started to sweat. My mind began to race. Everything within me reacted and started to shut down.

My soul's protectors and managers went into overdrive as I conjured every excuse why I couldn't—or wouldn't, or shouldn't—make this jump. My gut reaction was to reason, logically, why this would not be wise for me or my family.

I felt it all at once, but I didn't say a word. I couldn't process the flood of emotions crashing through me.

I just... shut down.

Have you ever felt like that? Your body reacts to something you're seeing or hearing, and you can't put words to why you're reacting.

I didn't want to jeopardize the opportunity by saying something foolish. I politely told Tomlin I would continue with the chaplain search process, but inside the idea was folding in on itself.

REAL MEN CRY?

I think many of us (especially men) have a hard time understanding our feelings. We may not even know what our true feelings are, let alone be vulnerable enough to express them. We may have even been raised to believe that feelings and vulnerability are a sign of weakness.

I was an emotional kid. I wore my feelings on my sleeve; they came to the surface whether I wanted them to or not.

In 1988, I was the ten-year-old quarterback of the Chippewa Indians football team. We were in the championship game against the Moon Tigers at Rochester High School stadium. It was a close game—in the fourth quarter, we were only up by one point, and our defense made a massive stand to prevent the Tigers from scoring a touchdown. We were backed up on our seven yard line. Moon still had all of their timeouts. If they stopped us from getting a first down, they'd get the ball back with enough time to score and win the game. All we needed to do was run the ball ten yards without a fumble, and then run out the clock.

My coach, Skip Haswell, called a time out. In the huddle, he called a quarterback sneak! He grabbed my facemask and said, "If you get hit, don't fight. Just go down. But if you see an opening, I want you to take it and run!"

I brought the team to the line of scrimmage, and the center hiked me the ball. I ran to the right, behind the guard, and then I saw an opening! I ran as fast as I could for an impressive seventy-five yards until Moon's Stan Reagan — I still remember his name — caught up and tackled me. I was disappointed that I didn't get the touchdown, but it didn't matter because the play sealed our championship!

The crowd went wild! I can still hear the cheers, cow bells, and plastic horns. My team jumped up and down along the sidelines and in the huddle. I approached the line of scrimmage. The center snapped me the ball and I took a knee to seal the win!

My teammates went crazy. Everyone was high-fiving, celebrating, but inside I felt this surge of emotion rising in my chest. Coach found me and offered his congratulations. I don't know what came over me, but I threw my arms around him, buried my head in his chest, and started to cry.

It was one of those ugly cries, a jumble of emotions I didn't know how to sort out as a ten-year-old. I was ecstatic, yet I was crying like a baby.

The tears poured out as my teammates congratulated me, and I suddenly felt embarrassed — I was the only one crying when everyone else was celebrating.

After all the excitement wore off, my dad found me in the crowd. He could sense my embarrassment, so he put both of his hands on my shoulder pads and said, "Son, look at me. Don't you ever forget this: real men cry."

That statement didn't sit right with me. I was confused by it, irritated. I rejected it — maybe because of our rocky relationship. Maybe because of his emotional outbursts (he suffered from bipolar disorder). Maybe because of my dad's actions that made my brother cry and eventually leave our home in order to live with his dad when I was only eight years old. Maybe because of the way he would peel out of the driveway in a fit of rage, leaving me standing there crying as he disappeared down the road.

Maybe I rejected his sentiment because I grew up in a culture that seemed to teach the exact opposite. The men I saw on TV and in movies didn't cry. Sports figures I admired never cried. I never saw my uncles or my coaches cry. The men I knew didn't cry. At least not that I ever saw.

The logical conclusion I made was, real men suck it up. Real men don't show that kind of emotion. Real men celebrate victory with chest bumps and high fives. They don't cry.

If a real man has those emotions, he pushes them down, and he pushes on.

PUSH 'EM DOWN!

Most of us have learned to push down our true feelings. We (especially men) have learned that we just don't discuss certain things. This leaves us feeling isolated, believing we're the only people in the world struggling.

Some of us speak openly about fears and other emotions. We're in an accountability group or a Bible study. But when certain topics or feelings make us uncomfortable, let's be honest… we shy away from talking about them. We don't go to "that" layer in our conversations; we avoid those types of "deep" discussions.

In my twenty-eight-year career as a pastor in the local church context and now in the NFL, I know this is true. People purposefully avoid this level of emotion and feelings.

I learned to do the same. I'd push down those types of feelings. If I felt like I was going to cry, I'd change the subject or leave the room. If I felt embarrassed, I learned to crack a joke or make fun of myself or someone else. If I felt any sort of negative emotions, I learned ways to ignore them, redirect them, or push them down.

Until I couldn't.

What I've learned over the years is that I can push those feelings down, but eventually they're going to come back up again, like submerging a beach ball in pool water. I could only hold my feelings down for so long before they'd eventually pop up with a big splash. My buried feelings would often erupt in ways I never intended and couldn't seem to control. Anger. Frustration. Irritation. Biting comments to my wife. Passive aggressive remarks at work. Popping off on my precious daughters. Yelling at people in other cars while in traffic.

I know I'm not the only one who struggles with this.

I wonder if you try to shove down your feelings. You think you're the only person who deals with that fear. Nobody else has that doubt. Nobody else can understand those feelings. Nobody else can relate to why you struggle. You feel like you're all alone, and you're afraid to tell someone what and how you really feel.

And that right there is Satan's strategy! Like a lion hunting its prey, the enemy of your soul wants to isolate you from others so he can pick you off and tear you apart. The devil wants you to feel all alone.

You have to see this.

FIGHT YOUR FEARS

The best way to fight against the darkness of isolation is to bring our fears into the light. There are other people in our lives who have struggled or are struggling with the feelings we're fighting against. The problem *seems* to be that nobody talks openly about that layer, so you and I must be bold enough to go there first. It doesn't feel natural, but we have to fight our hesitation on this one.

We need to take the leap to confide in trusted people with what we're truly feeling.

This is what Erica and I did when we were making the critical decision to join the staff of AIA. We talked at length with each other and God about our fears of raising our salaries and becoming full-time missionaries. It didn't go very well last time. We were afraid of leaving our comfortable roles to start something new. The last time we jumped like this, we hit the rocks — and still walk with a limp.

We were anxious about the unknown of doing ministry in the NFL. What if we crash and burn again?

We openly discussed these fears and more with our circle of trust (our mentors and close friends) and sought their wise counsel. We discovered that our fears were natural. Our friends and mentors had "been there and done that" themselves, and encouraged us to trust God and do it afraid.

"I BELIEVE. HELP MY UNBELIEF."

Recorded in Mark 9 is an incredible account of a *real* man bringing his fear and doubt into the light. A dark spirit had caused his son to be mute and suffer from seizures, so this dad brought his son to Jesus to be healed.

Mark wrote: "They brought the boy to him. And when the spirit saw him [Jesus], immediately it convulsed the boy, and he fell on the ground and rolled about, foaming at the mouth. And Jesus asked his father, "How long has this been happening to him?" And he said, "From childhood. And it has often cast him into fire and into water, to destroy him. But if you can do anything, have compassion on us and help us." And Jesus said to him, "'If you can!' All things are possible for one who believes." Immediately the father of the child cried out and said, "I believe; help my unbelief!" (Mark 9:21–24).

This *real* man cried! He cried out! He confessed his feelings to Jesus — he was afraid the spirit would eventually kill his son. He believed Jesus could do something about it, but he still had his doubts. His belief in Jesus' ability to heal his son was impacted by his fear and doubt. He made a true confession of his belief, but he brought those feelings of unbelief to Jesus.

You and I need to follow this guy's example.

REAL MEN CRY OUT!

The more I think about what my dad said, the more I realize how God has helped me to understand my feelings and emotions. It's been almost forty years since my dad spoke those words to me, and I have never forgotten them, just like he said. I now understand that he was teaching me a valuable life lesson: *Don't be afraid to express what you're feeling to God and those who are for you.*

I didn't understand it then, but I do now. If you've ever heard me preach, you know they call me the Crying Pastor! If you've ever grabbed coffee with me, you know I still wear my feelings on my sleeve and through my tear ducts. If you're in my circle of trust, you've heard me express my feelings and fears a lot. I've learned to not hold them back.

Never be afraid to express your fears. Discuss what makes you anxious with the people who care for you. Use wisdom as your filter and share your doubts, your struggles. Everyone has them, and we need to start normalizing the need to talk about them.

Bring those dark feelings of fear into the light. It's when we express our fears to God and others that the dark powers of fear must loosen its grip and come out of us. It's when we express our fears to Jesus that He can show us how His power is made perfect in our weakness.

What if the dad in Mark 9 was too afraid to bring his son to Jesus? What if his feelings kept him from trusting Jesus with his son?

We can only imagine…

But look at this! Mark documented that "he [Jesus] rebuked the unclean spirit, saying to it, 'You mute and deaf spirit, I command you, come out of him and never enter him again.' And after crying out and convulsing him terribly, it came out, and the boy was like a corpse, so that most of them said, 'He is dead.' But Jesus took him by the hand and lifted him up, and he arose" (Mark 9:25–27 [ESV]).

BOOM! That is the power of Jesus!

Because this *real* man brought his son and cried out his feelings of fear and doubt to Jesus, the boy was set free. Jesus lifted him up. His son rose and went on to live.

But I need you to see this…

The boy was not the only one transformed that day! Think about this dad. His weak belief turned into a stronger belief. His fears were silenced as his son began to speak again! His doubts were dashed in the presence of Almighty Jesus.

The dad's life was also radically transformed. The same thing can be true for you today.

Bring your doubts and fears into the open. Express those feelings to God and your inner circle of trust who will point you to Jesus. Fight back against Satan's destructive strategy to keep you isolated in your fear and get comfortable talking about what makes you uncomfortable.

See Satan's lie of unexpressed fear for what it is… a lie. Learn to fight back with the truth of God's word.

Unconfessed fear can keep you from seeing God's power at work in your life. Unexpressed fear can rob you of your God-given potential and purpose. Fear that goes unspoken can not only hijack what God has for you, but it could potentially steal what God has for future generations.

You never know how your boldness to come to Jesus with your doubts and fears might change the trajectory of your family and future generations, causing them to rise and truly live! So, express your fears, and watch what God can do with them.

My dad went to Heaven on June 21, 2024. I dedicate this chapter to him.

Dad, thanks for pointing me to Jesus and sharing this valuable life lesson with me. I've never forgotten it, and I understand what you were trying to say. Now I'm sharing that lesson with everybody. See you soon!

CHAPTER 10

Ask For Wisdom

*"We are to get wisdom and understanding,
yet we are not to lean on it apart from the Lord."*
John C. Maxwell

*"If any of you lacks wisdom, you should ask God,
who gives generously to all without finding fault,
and it will be given to you."*
James 1:5

*"...let the wise listen and add to their learning,
and let the discerning get guidance..."*
Proverbs 1:5

Hey, Siri! It might be one of my most repeated phrases in a day. Sad but true. Hey, Siri! What's the weather today? Hey, Siri! What are my next three calendar appointments? Hey, Siri! Who do the Steelers play this week?

We can ask Siri anything we want through our iPhones, and within seconds she'll regurgitate millions of well researched data points to answer our questions. If we don't know how to do something, many of us turn to YouTube to show us the way. Many high school and college students are even asking AI to do their research.

The advancements of technology are absolutely amazing! But at the same time, the rapid progression of available information is causing us to miss out on something we crucially need.

Wisdom.

In our world today, wisdom is in short supply. We have all the information we could ever want at our fingertips, but what we really need is wisdom. We can ask AI anything we want and it will pump out well studied data, but what we really need to navigate the decisions of life is wisdom. ChatGPT regurgitates facts, but it will never be able to give us what we really need: wisdom.

Information is cold, hard facts. Wisdom is lessons shared over hot coffee.

Information is shared in a search engine. Wisdom is given and received through shared experience.

Information is discoverable data. Wisdom is revealed truth deposited deep in our hearts.

Information is trivia answers for playing Jeopardy. Wisdom is soul-deep guidance for navigating life.

———

Solomon, son of David, the King of Israel, began the book of Proverbs by writing, "Hear, my son, your father's instruction, and forsake not your mother's teaching" (Proverbs 1:7 [ESV]). It's a relational invitation to sit at the feet of lived experience. Solomon was inviting his son (and us) to heed the wisdom of his successes and his failures.

Solomon invites us to "know wisdom and instruction, to understand words of insight, to receive instruction in wise dealing, in righteousness, justice, and equity; to give prudence to the simple, knowledge and discretion to the youth—let the wise hear and increase in learning, and the one who understands obtain guidance, to understand a proverb and a saying, the words of the wise and their riddles. The fear of the Lord is the beginning of knowledge; fools despise wisdom and instruction" (Proverbs 1:1–6 [ESV]).

Throughout Proverbs, Solomon shared with his son (and us) the lessons he learned along the way. Just in these first seven verses alone, he imparts a crucial lesson inspired by the Holy Spirit that we would be wise to apply in our lives, especially when we're making tough decisions: *seek wisdom.*

Solomon's invitation leads us to seek the wisdom of God and those who are in awe of Him.

START WITH GOD

The "fear of the Lord" can be a confusing phrase. What does Solomon mean? Are we supposed to be afraid of God? Dave Buehring shared this definition with me: *The fear of the Lord is reverencing and referencing God.*

Reverence

To revere God is to be in awe of Him. To worship Him with your whole being (heart, soul, mind, and strength). To revere God is to respect His vastness to the point of submitting your whole self under his greatness. To hold God in the highest esteem is to understand that He is all-powerful, all-knowing, and ever-present. To revere the Lord means you recognize that Almighty God holds your life in His hands and with one word could end it.

Niagara Falls comes to mind when I think of reverence. Those waterfalls are so beautiful and majestic. They are a tremendous sight to behold.

However, you better respect their sheer power. The strong force of the rushing water could take your life.

Reverencing God is to behold Him and recognize His greatness. The Scriptures teach us that we, as humans, cannot even behold the fullness of His glory or we would die. The Bible captures a friendly exchange between God and Moses about this.

Moses said, "Please show me your glory." And he said, "I will make all my goodness pass before you and will proclaim before you my name 'The Lord.' And I will be gracious to whom I will be gracious, and will show mercy on whom I will show mercy. But," he said, "you cannot see my face, for man shall not see me and live" (Exodus 33:18-20 [ESV]).

God is so big, so strong, and so mighty! There's nothing God cannot do that He wants to do. We are so fragile, pitiful, and weak compared to God. We cannot even look at His face and live.

This is what it means to posture ourselves in reverence and fear of the Lord.

Reference

To reference God is to submit your entire life under His Lordship. Solomon captures this perfectly: "Trust in the Lord with all your heart, and do not lean on your own understanding. In all your ways acknowledge him, and he will make straight your paths. Be not wise in your own eyes; fear the Lord, and turn away from evil" (Proverbs 3:5-7 [ESV]).

As followers of Jesus, we follow His lead. We do what the Holy Spirit reveals to us. We do life God's way, not ours. We die to our own opinions, and we refer to God's ways, the way Jesus lived his life, and we act accordingly. We study the Word of God to understand God's patterns of behavior, and we emulate His ways. We do not take our cues from the way our current culture operates. We follow Jesus' ways always. We constantly come back to God's ancient paths.

Jeremiah 6:16 (NIV) records: This is what the Lord says: "Stand at the crossroads and look; ask for the ancient paths, ask where the good way is, and walk in it, and you will find rest for your souls." To refer to God is to ask Him for the ancient paths on your current circumstances. God has a specific way He wants you to go. God has the best path for you to take. Referencing God is to fight your selfishness and do what He tells you to do.

Are you at a crossroads right now? Ask God for His wisdom.

James, the brother of Jesus said, "If any of you lacks wisdom, you should ask God, who gives generously to all without finding fault, and it will be given to you" (James 1:5 [ESV]). God promises to give you wisdom when you ask Him.

You might be thinking, how do I ask God for wisdom? What does that look like? How do I know if and when God answers? How do I know it's God's voice and not my own opinion or others?

We'll cover those answers in depth in the following chapters, but I'll say this. When you ask God for wisdom, wait. Listen for Him to speak before you move. The temptation is to move before God tells you to move, and moving too quickly could lead you to destruction (Been there. Done that.) God has various ways of speaking (Scripture, people, circumstances, songs, etc.), and it might take days, weeks, months, or years for you to really hear God's direction. Remember, it took me three years before I had the clarity from God that I needed to jump.

It's really important that you wait and listen for His still small voice while you're at a crossroads. God will reveal His ways to you in His timing. Be patient. When God does speak, take His path. God's ancient ways might not make sense to our current culture, but you can trust that His ways are everlasting. Refer to His ways, and you'll withstand the fire. Reference His ways, and you'll never be steered wrong. Submit to God's ancient ways because His path is always the best path in your current circumstances.

My prayer for you comes from Isaiah 30, as you continue to read the following chapters.

"So, the Lord must wait for you to come to him so he can show you his love and compassion. For the Lord is a faithful God. Blessed are those who wait for his help. O people of Zion, who live in Jerusalem, you will weep no more. He will be gracious if you ask for help. He will surely respond to the sound of your cries. Though the Lord gave you adversity for food and suffering for drink, he will still be with you to teach you. You will see your teacher with your own eyes. Your own ears will hear him. Right behind you a voice will say, "This is the way you should go," whether to the right or to the left" (Isaiah 30:18–21 [NLT]).

Ask God for wisdom. Wait for Him to speak.

THE WISDOM OF YOUR CIRCLE

As he opened the book of Proverbs, Solomon encouraged his son to seek the wisdom of God through others who have gone before us on the path. He then went on to share the godly wisdom that he had learned from God along the way.

A great way to seek God's wisdom is to ask others in your circle who are in awe of Him. Ask mentors who are also chasing Jesus for their wisdom as you stand at the crossroads. Ask trusted friends who you know will not just give you their opinion but the truth of God's word. Ask your pastor or small group leader and weigh their counsel against God's wisdom in the Scriptures.

When Erica and I were making the decision to jump on staff with AIA, we met with our mentors, pastors, and close friends. Their wise counsel caused us to consider things we hadn't even thought about. Their godly perspective challenged and increased our faith. We met with our friends who are MLB and NHL chaplains, which are similar roles to ours. Their godly wisdom caused us to ask some clarifying questions of Tomlin and the leadership of AIA. The wisdom of our trusted circle gave us incredible perspective as we considered making the jump.

It is wise to ask others for their wisdom when you're making big decisions. Who is in your circle of trust that will point you to God's ways? Who, when you ask them, will not just give you their opinion, but will point you to Jesus' example and His mission in that decision? Who will challenge you and not just go along with whatever you want? You need these types of people to get in your face and lovingly say the hard things you need to hear.

Who is in *your* circle of trust?

When it comes to making these big decisions, I would encourage you to keep your circle of trust tight. By doing this, you will avoid your potential decision leaking to people you don't want to know just yet. You want to choose only a few people you know will not blab your business with others. Choose those few trusted voices and fight the temptation to share your crossroads moment with a whole bunch of people. You never know how that information, in the wrong mouths, might lead to unnecessary conversations, distractions, or lost opportunities.

Open doors of gossip can shut doors of opportunity. Be careful, and keep your circle of trust very small.

My circle of trust was four guys and two couples. I explained our crossroads to this small but mighty wisdom counsel. My circle was: My mentor. My pastor who was also my boss. My former pastor. My best friend who is also a pastor. A mentor couple. Friends who are MLB/NHL chaplains. This group gave Erica and me a strong, well-rounded circle of trust, who we knew would point us to God's path.

Who is in *your* circle of trust?

My guess is that if you're still reading this chapter, you need some wisdom. You might have a circle of trust to reach out to regarding your decision or just life in general. Get together with them in the next few days and seek that wisdom together.

However, maybe you don't have that circle of trust. Here's my encouragement to you. Take a risk and ask someone you admire who is following Jesus the way you want to some day. Find the courage to ask someone who has stood at a similar crossroads to the one you're standing at right now. DM him. Email her. Ask a church leader to connect you with someone in a similar circumstance. Offer to treat that person to coffee or lunch. If he or she says yes, then come prepared to ask good questions. Take a ton of notes and then follow up with a thank you.

I know that a cold ask like that might be intimidating. I know you might feel uncomfortable to ask a new person to give you their wisdom. You have to fight that awkwardness. Take the risk. What's the worst thing that could happen?

I'll tell you. The worst thing is that you could miss out on that person being delighted to have a conversation with you and sharing their successes and failures with you. You could miss out on some Holy Spirit-led nuggets of wisdom that only that person has for you. You could make a stupid decision that could have been avoided by asking that person. That's what.

I know it's scary to ask someone to share a meal and their wisdom with you. It will be awkward. It will be out of your comfort zone.

I get it, but you need to get over it.

Heed the wisdom of Solomon. Don't be a fool by asking AI. Ask a real person with lived experience.

Do it afraid.

CHAPTER 11

P.R.A.Y. Through It

"Prayer should not be merely an act, but an attitude of life."
Billy Graham

*"Do not be anxious about anything, but in every situation,
by prayer and petition, with thanksgiving, present your requests
to God. And the peace of God, which transcends
all understanding, will guard your hearts and
your minds in Christ Jesus."*
Philippians 4:6-7

I'm a professional "pray-er." At least that's what most people think. When I was a local church pastor, I was always assigned to lead prayers before, during, and the end of worship services. I'm always asked to pray before meals at family gatherings. As an NFL chaplain, I begin and end chapels and Bible studies with prayer. Players ask me to pray for them before a game. A few minutes before kickoff, I bend the knee and grab the hand of a coach or player, and we pray the Lord's Prayer together. After every game, I gather with coaches and players from both teams at the fifty yard line to deflect the glory to God with a closing prayer.

Tomlin expects me to pray in the locker room after every game, win or lose. I pray a lot — professionally.

Believe me, I love the privilege of praying like this! But prayer is so much deeper than words being spoken out loud before a meal or after a game. Prayer is not just for professionals or the hyper spiritual. Prayer is for everyone.

Prayer is for you too.

When it's just me and God, I'm not a professional "pray-er." When I strip away the expectations of the pastoral profession, I'm just a vulnerable man who is still learning the power and posture of prayer. I'm learning the depths of this spiritual practice.

Praise. Reflection. Silence. Adoration. Asking. Listening. Personalizing certain prayers in Scripture over my life and for others. Sometimes, I just sit and think about God and the truth from His word that He brings to my mind. Other times, I don't even know what to say to God, and I just cry. That's prayer.

Prayer in its simplest form is relationship. Prayer is connection with God. Prayer is conversation with God. A good relational conversation goes two ways. Talking and listening. Many of us understand the talking part of praying, but we haven't learned the discipline of quieting ourselves long enough to hear God's reply (Psalm 46:10). We know we should make our requests known to God (Philippians 4:6), but we don't wait or look for His answer before we move on. Prayer is not a monologue. It's a dialogue. While I believe this to be 100 percent true, I also know that prayer is still so much deeper than this.

In 1 Thessalonians 5:17, the Apostle Paul encouraged the church to "pray without ceasing." What did he mean? Are we supposed to park ourselves in a church pew and spend all hours of the day praying? If so, when do you sleep and eat? Maybe you can pray while you're eating, but can you pray while you're sleeping? Are we supposed to lock ourselves in our prayer closet, away from all other things? Are we supposed to go throughout the day repeating the Lord's Prayer? What does Paul mean by this encouragement to pray without ceasing?

Prayer is a posture. Prayer is a lifestyle. Prayer is a mindset. Prayer is the recognition of your complete dependence on the Divine. Prayer is an attitude of the heart in every circumstance, aware of your human limitations and absolute reliance upon God yet simultaneously experiencing His grace and delight for being His child. Prayer is complete access to God's heart at any place and any time. Prayer is an open-handed posture of constant invitation for God to have His way and invade your life at will. If I can put it this way, prayer is your life's Bluetooth that is connected to God's wireless.

Before that tough meeting, prayer is the whisper under your breath asking for God's help as you enter the room. Prayer is inviting God to give you spiritual eyes while you're in that meeting. Prayer is listening for God's voice amidst the competing voices in that meeting. Prayer is being aware of God's movement within the room and discerning His still small voice as another person is speaking.

Before your workday, prayer is a continuous dedication of your work to the Lord. As you commune with God while you work, prayer is working "with sincerity of heart, fearing the Lord. Whatever you do, work heartily, as for the Lord and not for men, knowing that from the Lord you will receive the inheritance as your reward. You are serving the Lord Christ" (Colossians 3:23-24 [ESV]). Prayer is an invitation for God to order your steps throughout the day while having your spiritual antennas up for Him to interrupt your plans with His.

I hope you're getting the picture by now. Prayer is an ongoing communication with the living God who desires to be in relationship with you. God desires to speak with you. He constantly invites you to a deeper relational understanding of who He is and what He is doing and wants to do in and through your life.

ERICA, THE PRAYER NINJA

Since this is a book about making big decisions and jumping into your God-given purpose, I want to speak to some of the powerful lessons on prayer that Erica and I have learned along the way. Sometimes we hit the landing zone and sometimes we hit the rocks. Through it all, we've discovered unique tools for prayerfully surrendering to God's call on our lives.

That's what L.E.A.P. is all about. Learning these tools transformed the trajectory of our lives — literally.

I also want to say this before I go any further. I have learned so much from my wife in this area. Erica is much better at this than I am. When it comes to the practice of prayer, it seems that God has given her a spiritual gift and fervor for intercession (prayerfully intervening for another) since she was a teenager. The prayers that she has prayed for me, our family, and future family have changed the trajectory of our lives and generations to come. Anyone who knows her recognizes this depth in her prayer life with God, even if they don't know what it is that sets her apart.

Erica is a prayer warrior! Have you ever heard someone pray publicly and recognize that person has a depth of relationship with God that you long for some day?

Have you heard someone pray out loud and be intimidated to go next? That's my wife. Her prayer game intimidates me — in a good way. I want to be like her and learn to pray how she prays.

I often describe Erica as a Prayer Ninja. She's slicing and dicing the powers of darkness away from people's lives in the quiet shadows of her war room, often without them even knowing. My wife prayer walks our city, and no one knows that she's partnering with God to bridge transformation with every step. My wife's journals are filled with silent cries of intercession as she actively jumps into the tumultuous spiritual waters to partner with God to rescue lives.

We should learn to be like Erica, the Prayer Ninja. It can be intimidating, but the good news is that she learned how to pray from prayer warriors who have gone before her. She's discovered new levels of relationship with God through prayer. She's gained new techniques on how to approach prayer. She *learned* prayer.

We can also learn how to do this:

Praying continually in all things because we recognize that God cares about every small detail of our lives. Praying, especially in big moments, because we recognize that He also cares about the life-altering decisions of our lives.

Before you jump into that big decision, I encourage you to take the posture of prayer without ceasing. It is the non-linear and constant combination of L.E.A.P.—P.R.A.Y.: letting God lead, expressing your fears/feelings, asking God for wisdom, praying for the Holy Spirit to confirm/deny your decision, reading and meditating on God's word, waiting for God's response while you actively serve, and yielding/surrendering your feelings to God's call.

This L.E.A.P. — P.R.A.Y. framework is ultimately a giant prayer posture of the surrendered life. This type of a prayer life is recognition that when you have a relationship with God by grace through faith in Jesus Christ, you have a lifeline that is always open to Him. It's a life that is constantly striving to please God in all you do while recognizing He loves you and is already pleased with you. It's a God-honoring posture of "not my will but yours be done" because you recognize that His will is always best for you. A person who is willing to L.E.A.P. is a person who is willing to give up everything to obey God's voice, no matter the cost.

PRAY THROUGH IT

Baseball was my favorite sport to play growing up. When I was a little guy, I remember my coaches teaching my team how to run the bases. We'd all line up at home plate and practice running to first base. My coach would say, "If you hit a ground ball, you don't run TO first base.

You run THROUGH first base." What he was teaching us was that if you run *to* the base, you'll ease up and slow down before you get to the base. He wanted us to run *through* the base at full speed, so that if it was a close throw to first, we'd beat the throw by running as fast as we could *through* the base and down to the right of the foul line.

Many sports teach this principle. In track, you run through the finish line in a race. The same thing is true in swimming… you swim through the wall. The same principle applies in football… you tackle through the ball carrier. It's true for tennis… you swing the racket through the ball.

In this way, sports can teach us a lot about praying *through* a decision.

A lot of people pray to get *to* a decision. Few people pray *through* a decision. Many people pray about a decision but slow down that prayer pace once they get *to* the decision. A lot of us pray *before* we make a decision. That's good, but there's so much more power to uncover when we pray *through* a decision.

Many will whisper a prayer for God to *bless* a decision they've already made. As we've already discussed, what God initiates, He permeates. That's what we're after here. For God to permeate the entire process. What would it look like to invite God's discernment, favor, and wisdom before, during, and after the decision-making process?

There's a massive difference between praying *to* a decision and praying *through* a decision.

In the remainder of this book, I want to show you how Erica and I have learned to pray through big decisions—and not just to get to big decisions. I want to show you a specific model we have learned to P.R.A.Y. that invites the Holy Spirit to be with us in and throughout the decision-making process. We have learned some special nuggets of wisdom in private conversations with our mentors that I want to make public because I think they can help you in your journey of jumping into your God-given purpose.

I want to help you hit your God-designed landing zone. I want to be the guy at the bottom of the cliff showing you how Erica and I jumped. I want to cheer you on by sharing these powerfully unique tools to help you hit your narrow landing zone.

I know there's a specific place where God's call will meet your obedience to jump and trust Him with your life. I know that's scary for you, but I also know that it's there that you will come alive in ways beyond your imagination. I hope and pray these following chapters will help you jump into the assignment and purpose God has for you, but I don't want you to just take my word for it as a "professional pray-er." I want you to take God's word for it as you pray.

Follow Jesus' example of praying *through* hard decisions.

Before Jesus launched his public ministry, he prayed *through* the devil's temptation in the wilderness by memorizing, recalling, and fighting back through Scripture (Matthew 4:1–11).

Jesus taught his disciples to pray through life's challenging circumstances through a life-changing model prayer (Matthew 6:9–13; Luke 11:2–4).

Jesus prayed *through* the night before he chose the twelve apostles (Luke 6:12-16). He continued to pray for them as he taught them and walked alongside them (Luke 22:31–32; John 17).

Jesus taught the explosive lesson of appropriately approaching God through prayer when he let his emotions show. He cleared the temple and shouted, "My house will be called a house of prayer, but you are making it a den of robbers" (Matthew 21:12–17; Mark 11:15–17; Luke 19: 45–46; John 2:13–17).

Jesus wept and prayed *through* the death of his friend, Lazarus, and by God's power, he raised Him back to life (John 11).

Jesus prayed all night *through* the anxiety as he weighed the decision to go to the cross (Matthew 26:36–56; Mark 14:32–52; Luke 22:40–53; and John 18:1–11). He willingly went through with it.

As Jesus was tortured and crucified, he prayed *through* the physical, mental, and emotional pain. As he hung on the tree of Calvary, he prayed to God to forgive the people who crucified him. Jesus expressed his feelings of being abandoned by God (Matthew 27:46). He cried out to God, "It is finished" (John 19:30). Jesus called out with a loud voice, "Father, into your hands I commit my spirit." When he had said this, he breathed his last (Luke 23:46).

Are you getting my point?

Prayer was a lifestyle for Jesus. Communion with God, His Father, was constantly on his heart. Prayer was his state of mind throughout his life and ministry. Jesus did what God told him to do (John 5:19). He prayed all the way *through* to the completion of his God-given purpose. As a result of Jesus praying through his mission, the world was transformed forever! Because of what Jesus prayed through and went through, your purpose (and mine) has been eternally changed.

Over the next few chapters, I want to point you to Jesus' example of praying through life's decisions and share the lessons I've learned from others who are also following His lead. I'm still learning these and doing my best to apply them to my life.

I'm praying for God to get through to you what you need to get to and through your God-given purpose. That's a bit of a tongue twister, but it's a power-packed sentence!

Read it slowly one more time. Now personalize it.

God, I'm praying for You to get through to me. Speak clearly to me. I will submit to whatever you want to do and need to do to get me to jump into my God-given purpose. Give me the courage and strength to jump and get through the highs and lows of my God-given calling.

Would you join me in praying *through* that sentence for your life before you move on?

CHAPTER 12

Prayer Runway

"Simply defined, prayer is earthly permission for heavenly interference."
Tony Evans

"Devote yourselves to prayer, being watchful and thankful."
Colossians 4:2

The plane suddenly dropped and so did my belly. It tilted quickly from side to side and so did my imagination. I heard the "ding" and saw the seatbelt sign light up, and my blood pressure went up. I couldn't wait to get on the ground. I hate turbulence.

The pilot came over the loudspeaker: "Ladies and gentlemen, we'll be circling for a bit until the runway is cleared for us to land." An incoming storm had grounded several planes, and they were backed up on the runway. Our plane couldn't land until the others were cleared. While we were up there circling, the turbulence was getting worse.

Sometimes making a big decision can feel like this. Your belly drops with worry and anxiety. Your imagination runs wild with all the different scenarios. Your patience is more than tested. When we feel the turbulence while trying to make the decision, we tend to rush it, forcefully land the plane, and get on with our lives.

What if there was a different way to land the decision plane?

IT SEEMED GOOD

The newly established Church was at a crossroads. Leadership had to make a tough decision: a major difference had surfaced as to how Jews and Gentiles would experience the free gift of salvation and follow Jesus. The turbulence leading up to the decision is recorded in Acts 15. (Take a few minutes and read it for yourself. Put yourself in the Gentile's sandals as you do. Ouch!)

The conflict cut back and forth. The council heard dialogue presenting different sides of the issue. The Pharisees weighed in with their strong opinion. Peter stood up and gave his rebuttal from God's Word. Paul and Barnabas shared eyewitness testimony of what God had done with the Gentiles. After hearing and weighing all the different voices, James—Jesus' brother and leader of the Jerusalem Council—stood up and declared the final decision. I want you to see how he communicated to everyone in a letter, explaining how they arrived at that major decision.

The letter said, "it has seemed good to us, having come to one accord, to..." and "it seemed good to the Holy Spirit and to us..." (Acts 15: 26, 28 [ESV]).

The Church leadership, being led by the Holy Spirit, moved forward in unity. As a result, they felt confident about their decision and communicating it to those who would be impacted.

But I need you to see something important.

Did you see the phrase, "it seemed good" in the Acts 15 letter? Did the Church leadership really decide based off an "it seemed good" moment?

Yes, they did.

Like turbulence, making big decisions can seem overwhelming at times. It can feel like everything hinges on YOU getting the decision right, like it all depends on YOU to land the plane safely on the runway. I know it seems that way, but...

What if it didn't have to be that way? What if it didn't have to depend solely on you?

Wouldn't that seem good to you?

I've learned a new way to land the decision plane that I want to share with you. I call it the *Prayer Runway*.

When Erica and I were trying to make the massive decision to jump on staff with AIA, Dave reminded me of a prayer strategy that clears the runway and gives room for the Holy Spirit to land on the decision. This prayer blueprint provided us with the confidence we needed to make the decision together. We moved forward in complete unity with one of the biggest decisions of our married life. After we rediscovered this *Prayer Runway*, it seemed good for us to make the jump.

That's what I want for you.

As you embrace the fear of the unknown in your decision, what would it look like for you to invite other trusted copilots to help you land the plane? What if you asked other people to pray with you through your decision so that it seems good in unity? What if you requested the Holy Spirit to land your decision so that you can be confident moving forward?

That's what Erica and I did. Let me show you how.

PRAYER CALENDAR

Most of the time, when making a big decision, we face a deadline. A job offer will only stand for so long before the company moves on. The position that came in our feed won't be there for long. Even the speed of the housing market can determine how quickly we need to decide to move.

Some of the time, when making a big decision, we get to choose our deadline: the jump from one career to another on our own terms; the rollout of a new vision and mission for the organization; the hiring or firing of team members.

Remember, we've talked about letting God lead the whole process. God permeates what He initiates, and what we initiate, we must sustain. We don't want to get ahead of God in the decision-making process, but there are times when God allows a deadline by which the decision must be made.

After Tomlin offered me the chaplain position in 2019, he gave me a decision deadline: two and a half weeks. That date on my calendar was Friday, July 12.

Erica and I got to work employing the L.E.A.P. framework. We had already begun discussing this possibility with our tight circle of trust, but when it became a formal offer, we scheduled conversations and prayer times with each of them. On certain days, we fasted from food, replacing mealtime with prayer. We prayed together and apart. She and I journaled our thoughts and prayers. Together, we sought the Lord's will for this big decision that needed to be made by July 12.

One of the most crucial steps — my mentor's advice — was to circle the date on the calendar, either physically or mentally.

Circle the day you have to communicate your decision. Back up that date by one week. Now circle that new date. As far as *it seems good* to you and your circle of trust, make the decision in your heart by then. But don't communicate it just yet.

July 5 was the day for Erica and me — the day we decided to become full-time missionaries... in our hearts.

Now here comes the *Prayer Runway*. During the next five days, rest. Invite the Holy Spirit to land your decision plane by confirming or denying your decision. Don't talk about the decision during those five days. Ask your circle of trust to keep praying. Keep your Bluetooth connected to the Holy Spirit's wireless as you read God's word and worship. In essence, you're giving intentional time and space for the Holy Spirit to breathe on your decision and land on your heart's runway. While your decision seems good to you, you want the moment where you can look back and know that the Holy Spirit truly landed.

Day six is crucial! This is the day before you communicate your decision out loud.

Day six is a day of confidence, the day you touch base with your circle of trust (and especially the people you're making the decision with) and ask them if the Holy Spirit whispered or shouted anything contrary to the decision you made in your heart six days ago.

Erica and I came back together on July 11 (our day six) and compared notes. There was nothing she noticed or heard that indicated the Holy Spirit was denying our decision to become full-time missionaries. Likewise, I hadn't sensed anything that suggested the Holy Spirit was denying us in accepting the offer to become the team chaplain of the Pittsburgh Steelers.

Because of this, *it seemed good* to us and the Holy Spirit that we should move forward. Thanks to the Prayer Runway, we were confident that God had called us into this, and He would be with us throughout the journey.

Day seven is powerful! It's the day you communicate your decision with confidence, knowing that God is with you. Day seven can also be the day you're certain that God doesn't want you to move forward. Either way, you can have confidence the Holy Spirit has guided you along the way.

On July 12, my day seven, I communicated to Tomlin that Erica and I were in, and told AIA leadership I was accepting the position.

Erica and I were confident that God had called us, but we still had human concerns. We had big faith, but still had some big fears.

Because of the *Prayer Runway*, our yes to God was louder than our fears.

GODFIDENCE

The *Prayer Runway* gives you confidence that God is in it or doesn't want you in it.

The *Prayer Runway* gives you confidence that God has gone before you, that God is with you in it, and that God will be with you through the completion of your purpose on the other side of that decision.

This is what former Steelers player Jordan Dangerfield calls GODfidence. One day at practice, I noticed his "GODfidence" tattoo. I asked him what it meant to him—you can learn a lot about a person when you ask about their tattoos. He said, "My confidence comes from God. When I put God in the first place, He puts everything else in the right place." Jordan believed that and lived by that.

This is what the *Prayer Runway* does. It gives you GODfidence.

When you invite the Holy Spirit to be central in your decision-making process, you can have GODfidence that He has led you and will put everything in the right place that God wants for you.

The next time you're faced with a big decision, invite the Holy Spirit to land your plane on His clear runway. Trust the Holy Spirit to be your pilot.

CHAPTER 13

Read God's Word

"You don't need new truth. You need a fresh revelation of what has always been real and always been true."
Winkie Pratney

"All Scripture is breathed out by God and profitable for teaching, for reproof, for correction, and for training in righteousness, that the man of God may be complete, equipped for every good work."
2 Timothy 3:16-17

In my early thirties, I was invited to have lunch with Dr. Henry Blackaby. He was a well-known pastor, ministry leader, and author. What a privilege for me as a young pastor to be invited to a private luncheon during the Conversations with the Fathers of the Faith event hosted in Pittsburgh by Dave Buehring and Lionshare Leadership Group. I was graciously seated directly across the table from this spiritual giant of small stature. I'd read several of his books and listened to many of his teachings. I was nervous yet excited to ask him to share his wisdom with me.

"Dr. Blackaby," I asked, "what advice would you give me as a young pastor in the city of Pittsburgh?" I expected him to download all kinds of lessons, tips, and tricks of the pastoral trade. I was ready to take notes to capture the almost six decades of spiritual leadership wisdom he would share with me over lunch.

Blackaby leaned forward. He looked directly at me and said, "Read your Bible and pray." Then he sat back in his chair, buttered his roll, and ate it.

"That's it?" I thought. "That's all you have for me?" There was an awkward silence as I waited for him to share more, but when I realized he wasn't I scrambled to find and ask my next question. By the time I gathered myself, someone else had engaged him in conversation. I had lost my moment, so I just listened to him drop serious wisdom on those around the table.

"Read your Bible and pray." It turns out that's all I needed. He dropped more advice in those five words than I realized.

The main way God speaks to people is through His Word. He has revealed His character, ways, and mission in the pages of this sacred text. The Bible is inspired by God. The Scriptures are used by the Holy Spirit to help us hear from Him. Digging into the Bible is absolutely essential to maturing in your faith and being equipped to step into God's calling on your life.

Read God's Word for yourself. We've talked about the importance of prayer in the previous two chapters. Now I want to highlight the monumental significance of intentionally and rhythmically reading and studying God's Word, especially as you consider jumping into your God-given purpose.

Paul wrote to a young pastor named Timothy, "All Scripture is breathed out by God and profitable for teaching, for reproof, for correction, and for training in righteousness, that the man of God may be complete, equipped for every good work" (2 Timothy 3:16-17).

I want to break down these two verses to help you understand their importance in helping equip you for the good work God has for you.

BREATHED OUT BY GOD

Scripture is divinely inspired. God breathed on (or supernaturally led) the forty-plus authors to write for a period of approximately 1500 years. The different books of the Bible were written at various times and places. Biblical writers dealt with a multitude of topics over several centuries, and God inspired a cohesive and harmonious narrative throughout all sixty-six books.

In Dave Buehring's A *Discipleship Journey*, he explains the Bible has endured more attacks by its enemies than any other book in all of history.

From the days of the Roman Empire until today, skeptics have tried to destroy its influence. Voltaire, one of France's greatest thinkers, once said that in a hundred years the Bible would be forgotten and copies only found in museums. History tells us that a hundred years after his death, the Geneva Bible Society used Voltaire's house as their headquarters and his press to mass-produce Bibles for the first time!

"No historical book has such a large number of surviving copies as the Bible. Written on perishable material and being hand-copied over and over again hundreds of years before the creation of the printing press did not lessen its existence or accuracy. The Jews had special groups of men whose sole responsibility was to preserve the Scriptures, making sure every paragraph, word, and letter was transmitted absolutely perfectly.

"The greatest proof of the supernatural power of the Scriptures is the testimony of the millions of lives that were radically changed as they encountered Jesus through it. Only the truths revealed in the Bible make bad people good on the inside, transforming rebels into servants of humility."

God's words were given through the authors supervised by the Holy Spirit. God chose to inspire the authors to reveal Himself without error to all of humanity throughout history.

What a gift from God to us!

PROFITABLE FOR TEACHING

Profitable means purposed. The intended purpose (or use) of the Scriptures is to teach God's truth, instructing believers in what is true about God's ways, character, and mission. All Scripture is inspired by God and is useful to teach what is true.

Truth, in our culture today, is up for personal definition. It was in Timothy's day too. That's why Paul reminds the young pastor that God's truth is not up for interpretation or negotiation.

Jesus said, "I am the truth" (John 14:6). God's truth is truth, and Timothy was to teach God's truth. We have to be careful not to just take any pastor's word for it. We have to test what is being taught as truth, and the only way to do that is to turn to God's truth.

"Studying the Bible is not primarily for information, but for the transformation of the heart. As the Scriptures reveal God's heart to us, we become more like Him. For example, we see Ezra studying God's truth (Ezra 7:10) and the Bereans (Acts 17:11) researching the Scriptures to make sure Paul had told the truth." (Buehring, 2022)

Please don't just take my word for it. Test everything I'm writing against the Bible. Don't take my word for it unless God's Word confirms it.

REPROOF

The Greek term translated as "reproof" or "rebuke" is elegmos, taken from the word elegcho, which can be translated "convict," "expose," or "bring to light." The truth of God's Word brings our sinful nature and actions into the light and make us realize what is wrong and why it's wrong. Reproof involves the Holy Spirit revealing a sin, fault, or mistake to someone, not to cause shame, but to guide them toward the better path of righteousness.

The Scriptures' purpose is to be a mirror for us. As we gaze into the truth of God's Word, we see our own faults and the unblemished character of Jesus in contrast. Scripture is used to rebuke by providing a clear standard for right and wrong in that mirror.

Our culture tries to set their own standard of right and wrong but in a way inconsistent with God's standard. The Bible's mirror invites us to repent of our sin, receive God's forgiveness, and rest in His grace that causes us to look more like Him each day. God kindly revealed in the mirror of Scriptures a standard that lead us to repentance.

CORRECTION

If reproof is the mirror, correction is our GPS (or directions app on your phone).

The Scriptures not only convict us, but they correct us when and where we're wrong. God was kind enough that when we do make a wrong turn, the Bible acts as our GPS. God, in His goodness, gave us instructions and examples to correct our sinful position and help recalculate our direction to get back on God's path and standard of righteousness.

As sinful as I am, I'm grateful for the mirror of reproof. I'm even more grateful for the GPS of correction. It would be awful to have the conviction of my sin without the right directions to correct my sinful actions. This is what the Bible does. It not only brings my sin out of the darkness of death, but it shows me the right way to move forward into the light of life.

TRAINING IN RIGHTEOUSNESS

Righteousness is the goal. Looking more like Jesus when we look in the mirror is the daily target. This doesn't happen overnight. We have to train ourselves to live in God's standard of righteousness. We do this by developing a daily discipline (or rhythm) of reading God's Word.

Paul loved to use imagery to help his readers understand his teaching. Recorded in 1 Corinthians 9:24-27 (NLT), Paul writes, "Don't you realize that in a race everyone runs, but only one person gets the prize? So run to win! All athletes are disciplined in their training. They do it to win a prize that will fade away, but we do it for an eternal prize. So, I run with purpose in every step. I am not just shadowboxing. I discipline my body like an athlete, training it to do what it should." Paul likens training for godly living to training to win a race.

The Greek term translated as "training" is paideian, literally meaning "child training." In context, Paul means that the purpose of the Scriptures is to guide new believers in God's ways. This is reminiscent to the words of the Shema recorded in Deuteronomy 6:4–9 (ESV), which says, "Hear, O Israel: The Lord our God, the Lord is one. You shall love the Lord your God with all your heart and with all your soul and with all your might. And these words that I command you today shall be on your heart. You shall teach them diligently to your children, and shall talk of them when you sit in your house, and when you walk by the way, and when you lie down, and when you rise. You shall bind them as a sign on your hand, and they shall be as frontlets between your eyes. You shall write them on the doorposts of your house and on your gates."

Training for righteousness, according to the Scriptures, has an ancient rhythm to it. We don't just train for one hour on Sunday morning. We train by developing multiple daily scriptural disciplines in our homes — before we go to bed, after we wake up, as we're walking, as we're talking, etc. We train like this to strengthen our ongoing relationship with God and

His standard of truth and righteousness. To run the race as a disciple of Jesus, we undertake a daily dedication to training, discipline, sacrifice, endurance, and focus. We don't do this to earn God's love and favor. We do this from an already established relationship with God through Jesus.

This training becomes our ambition as we seek to live out our God-given purpose, and produces fruit in and through our lives. As we attach ourselves to Jesus in multiple rhythms, we will grow in our relationship with God and His righteousness.

"As we develop our relationship with God through Scripture, worship, prayer, guarding our hearts, and giving generously, we will reap the wonderful fruit of knowing God even better. As God's Word promises, discipline will produce a harvest of righteousness and peace for those who have been trained by it (Hebrews 12:1-11)." (Buehring, 2022)

COMPLETE, EQUIPPED FOR EVERY GOOD WORK

When we make the time to read, study, and apply the Bible, God promises us that we will be complete, equipped for every good work. We will be complete (meaning capable and skilled) in the sense of being able to meet all the demands that will come our way.

Doesn't that sound like exactly what you need as you consider jumping into your God-given purpose? To have the skill and character necessary to accomplish the task(s) at hand. To have the words to say at the exact right moment. To be qualified for the call God has on your life. When the fear begins to grip your heart, this is exactly what you need to remember. God qualifies you for what He calls you to do.

To drive home his point even further, Paul added the Greek word exērtismenos, which means "equipped." This word means to be "furnished" like a fully furnished apartment—you don't need anything else. It comes fully stocked and decked out with God's power and purpose. With the living and active Scriptures (see Hebrews 4:12) in your heart, soul, and mind, you have all that you need for the work God is calling you to do.

Paul was reminding the young pastor of the incredible gift of the Scriptures that he was given. This would have been such a confidence boost for Timothy. Paul was confident of Timothy's commitment to and dependence on the Scriptures, and he was even more confident of God's ability to supply all Timothy's needs through God's Word.

THE BIRDS CAME ALIVE!

As Erica and I were trying to make the decision to join the staff of AIA, we committed ourselves to reading God's Word. We read it separately. We read it together. We were in a weekly small group to study God's Word. We went to worship services where we heard the Bible preached. Bible reading was (and is) a part of our regular rhythm.

It made sense that God's Word came alive to us when we saw the baby birds being fed by their mom and protected by their dad (see Chapter 5). The very words of Jesus, freshly recommitted to our memories, came to fruition right in front of our eyes. Jesus said, "Look at the birds of the air. They do not sow or reap or store away in barns, and yet your Heavenly Father feeds them. Are you not much more valuable than they?" (Matthew 6:26 [NIV]).

This highlighted truth jumped off the pages of the Bible and sealed the calling of God deep into our hearts.

Because God's Word literally came alive through those birds, we had the confidence to jump.

God's Word was a gift that day.

The same can be true for you. As you embrace the fear of the unknown, I am confident of God's ability to supply you with everything you need to make the jump. God has given you an amazing gift in the pages of the Bible. My encouragement to you is to create a daily discipline, a regular rhythm, of reading God's Word.

Here's why: consistency in God's Word allows more opportunity for God to reveal Himself and His plans for your life. Remember, the main way God speaks to us is through His Word.

I realize that reading the Bible can be intimidating. It can be a very confusing book if you don't know how to read it. If you're new to it, I'd like to help you by giving you a simple teaching outline that I have created and used for the last several years when teaching people how to read the Bible for the first time.

HOW DO I STUDY THE BIBLE?

Before you even begin...

TRANSLATION: Which trusted version should I use? (I recommend English Standard Version)

TIME: What will be my rhythm? (Morning? Lunch hour? Evening?)

TEAM: Who can read with me? (Iron sharpens iron - Proverbs 27:17)

As you read...

1. OBSERVE: What it simply says

   - Ask the comprehension questions: Who? What? When? Where? Why? How?

2. INTERPRET: What it originally meant

   Context is King!

   - What is the cultural and/or historical context of this passage?
   - What else do I know about the book, author, and broader context of the passage?

Scripture Interprets Scripture

- What other Scripture passages might help me better interpret this one?
- Allow the Bible to help you understand other passages of the Bible. Where similar words are used, explore the context of each of those instances.

Ask the Holy Spirit for Help

For the Spirit searches everything, even the depths of God. For who knows a person's thoughts except the spirit of that person, which is in him? So also no one comprehends the thoughts of God except the Spirit of God. Now we have received not the spirit of the world, but the Spirit who is from God, that we might understand the things freely given us by God. And we impart this in words not taught by human wisdom but taught by the Spirit, interpreting spiritual truths to those who are spiritual. (1 Corinthians 2:10-13 [ESV])

Avoid...

- Twisting it to mean what you want it to mean
- Google searches, ChatGPT, and social media for interpretations

3. APPLY: What I do with it

- Once we know what it means, we can now ask, "What does this mean for me?"
- What does this teach me about God, and what does this now show me about myself?
- What does God want me to do as a result?

RESOURCES

As you're maturing in your faith, I want to recommend to you two resources that have completely transformed my Bible reading, Scriptural understanding, and spiritual growth.

A DISCIPLESHIP JOURNEY by Dave Buehring — lionshare.org

A *Discipleship Journey* (ADJ) is a resource created to equip followers of Jesus to grow spiritually while being empowered to make disciples that make disciple makers. Whether it is grounding a young believer in core biblical truths or shoring up the foundations of veterans of the faith, this interactive resource leads Jesus followers through a dozen key discipleship themes over the course of a year. ADJ is a practical guide to make disciple makers! Each chapter builds on the one before to lead believers to an understanding of how what they have learned can be passed on and invested in others. There are twelve themes covered in this manual, or as some have called it "a handbook for the Bible."

- Knowing God
- A Call to Discipleship
- The Grace of God
- The Cross, Sin and Repentance
- Hearing the Voice of God
- The Disciple's Disciplines
- Relationships
- Spiritual Warfare
- The Church in Acts
- Advancing the Kingdom
- Purpose, Passion and Gifts
- Making Disciple Makers

This resource has transformed my life. I have walked with hundreds of men over the years using the Bible and this practical tool as our guide, and I've watched God transform each of them at some point during their discipleship journey. As a result of intentional time in the Scriptures using A *Discipleship Journey*, I've seen marriages restored, families strengthened, and careers shifted. Because this was birthed out of a heart to co-mission with Jesus, God has His hand on this resource in a powerful way.

MISSION 119 by Pastor John Soper — mission119.org

Mission 119 is a free online and mobile Bible study tool created by Pastor John Soper to help people develop a daily habit of Bible engagement, deepen their understanding of scripture, and apply its truths to their lives. Named after the Bible's longest chapter, Psalm 119, it provides guided daily readings, audio commentaries, and quizzes to facilitate transformation and growth in believers. Psalm 119:11 (NIV) says, "I have hidden your word in my heart that I might not sin against you."

This is a powerful Bible reading plan. It's a ninety-one week journey through the entire Bible. It will help you develop the habit of daily Bible study, encouraged and assisted by Pastor Soper's brief, but insightful audio commentary. The program encourages you to apply biblical truths and experience spiritual growth and transformation. You can also answer questions and take quizzes to enhance your understanding and retention of Scripture.

What I love about Mission 119 is the length. It gives you attainable reading goals for each day with the weekend off to catch up if you get behind. Other plans to read through the whole Bible gave me too much to read, and I could not comprehend everything I was reading. I also love the Pastor Soper's 10-10 approach. It's ten minutes of reading and/or listening to the Scriptures and ten minutes of listening to him explain what I just read. I need that, and I appreciate him for creating this powerful tool.

If I were to offer you some advice as you consider jumping into your God-given purpose, it would be the same advice Dr. Henry Blackaby gave to me.

Read your Bible and pray.

With those five words, you'll have everything you ever need to make the jump. In fact, you'll have everything you ever need.

CHAPTER 14

Active Waiting

"God's timing is just as important as His direction."
Dave Buehring

"Wait for the Lord; be strong, and let your heart take courage; wait for the Lord!"
Psalm 27:14

Our culture hates to wait.

Think about fast food. Restaurants once competed for the quickest drive-thru times, but now many have bypassed the drive thru altogether in favor of mobile orders with zero wait. If people have to wait even a minute to pick up their mobile order, they get upset.

Think about internet speed. We get frustrated when our device takes longer than one second to deliver the information we want. One second! Whenever my streaming service buffers on my smart TV for just a few seconds, I get flustered.

Anybody else?

Think about the immediacy of shopping. You can hit "purchase" on your mobile device, and what used to take weeks to ship now shows up at the door within a day or even within the hour. If it takes longer than two days for an item to ship across the ocean, people are ready to file a complaint or fight for free shipping.

Our culture doesn't know how to wait. Our culture has no category for what it's like to wait for anything anymore. We live in an "instant" culture. This is one of the reasons why we struggle when God makes us wait.

TRAFFIC LESSON

I hate traffic. I try to avoid it all costs. I plan my commute around it, even if it means going into work ninety minutes early to avoid sitting in it. I take alternate routes to bypass the congestion. I can't stand the stop-start, stop-start, stop-start. I despise wasting expensive gas. And the long lineup of cars crawling along hinders me from getting to my destination quickly.

I just want to get where I'm going as soon as possible.

The problem is traffic is unavoidable for me. It's inevitable for my commute into and through the city of Pittsburgh. It will be there whether I want it or not. But I've learned a valuable spiritual lesson from sitting in it throughout the years.

Repurpose the wait.

I've learned to leverage the wait. I now schedule phone meetings. I chat with my mom and sister as I slowly make my way home. I call my buddies to catch up on life as I follow the car in front of me. I listen to my church's sermons that I missed because I was out of town with the team. I listen to leadership podcasts while I inch along at a snail's pace. I'll turn on worship songs and sing at the top of my lungs instead of yelling at the guy who just cut me off.

Does any of that get me to my destination faster? No, but it has done something in my heart and mind while I wait to get there. Do I get to work faster? No, but repurposing the wait has grown my relationship with the Lord and others. Do I get home quicker by doing all these things? No, but God has done a lot of work in my heart as I connect with Him and others.

This is the spiritual principle of *active waiting*.

HURRY UP AND WAIT

The most frustrating part of my "Do It Afraid" story was the wait. I knew in my knower that God was moving me on to something new. I didn't know what it was or when I would get there, but I knew I was going somewhere. God had me in stand-still traffic for almost three years! From the time I felt that first nudge to the moment I received the clarity to jump, three years had passed filled with invaluable lessons in repurposing the traffic.

Maybe you're waiting in life's traffic right now as you read this book. You know God has called you to something, but you're not exactly sure if the timing is right. Maybe you have a dream that is within your grasp, but you're waiting on God to open the right door. Maybe you know the *where*, but you're waiting on the *when*.

I want to remind you of what my mentor said to me. "God's timing is just as important as His direction." I know that can be frustrating to hear right now but trust me when I say that God's timing is always perfect. He's never late. He'll get you there when He wants you there. Draw near to Him in the traffic. Follow His lead, and He'll signal to you when it's time to change lanes and move forward.

I know how hard it is to wait for God's timing! I'm as impatient in life as I am in traffic. But just like my traffic lesson, I learned to repurpose the wait. I want to encourage you to do the same.

What would it look like for you to intentionally repurpose your wait?

How can you draw closer to Him while you wait? How can you worship God as you wait? How can you purposefully wait on the Lord as the Scriptures invite you to do?

If *active waiting* is a new concept to you, I'd suggest five different ways to practice, which we used while waiting on God at different times in our marriage and ministry. I encourage you to quickly put one (or all of them) into practice as you wait. Hurry up and wait!

PRAYER RETREATS

Schedule some time to get alone with God. Get it on your calendar and block it out. Make the time.

If you're married, you can take your spouse with you. If you have kids, don't take them with you. Invest in a trusted babysitter to watch over those wonderful distractions.

Go away to a place that will allow you to seek God and rest in His presence. For me, that's in the woods. It's more glamping (glamorous camping) — a nice cabin with a view of nature where I can walk in the woods. That might not be restful for you, so figure out your style and get away to that place.

Psalm 46:10 says, "Be still, and know that I am God." James 4:8 says, "Draw near to God, and He will draw near to you." This is the reason for the prayer retreat. To be still. To draw near to God. Simply be with God and tend to your relationship. Share your heart with Him in prayer. Invite God into your waiting by asking Him for wisdom and then being quiet long enough for Him to speak to you in that still small voice or gentle whisper (see 1 Kings 19:12).

Erica and I have learned this practice from our mentors. We've prioritized getting away separately with God and together with God. We financially plan for these prayer retreats and see it as an investment in our marriage, ministry, and relationship with God. Each time Erica and I have carved out time for a prayer retreat, we have left unified with fresh confirmation of God's direction and have committed to wait for His timing.

MINI MONUMENTS

Throughout the Scriptures, you'll see that leaders marked certain significant moments by building monuments to actively remember what God had done. For example, when God miraculously delivered the Israelites from the hand of the Philistines, we see how "Samuel took a stone and set it up between Mizpah and Shen. He named it Ebenezer, saying, "Thus far the Lord has helped us" (1 Samuel 7:12).

In Joshua 4 we read about the miracle of how God parted the waters of the Jordan River for the people of Israel to crossover on dry ground. God commanded Joshua to take twelve stones from the riverbed and pile them up in the Promised Land at Gilgal. The stones served as a visual, physical reminder of God's divine intervention. They represented the unity of the twelve tribes of Israel and testified to God's power and commitment to keep His promises.

Jesus instituted another kind of monument. We see Him build it at the Last Supper. Paul writes about it in 1 Corinthians 11:23–25 (ESV) "For I received from the Lord what I also delivered to you, that the Lord Jesus on the night when he was betrayed took bread, and when he had given thanks, he broke it, and said, "This is my body, which is for you. Do this in remembrance of me." In the same way also he took the cup, after supper, saying, "This cup is the new covenant in my blood. Do this, as often as you drink it, in remembrance of me."

I think it's important to follow their examples by building mini monuments.

Mini monuments help us remember when and how God intervened, and they cause us to live with the hope that He can and will do it again. We remember God's faithfulness and we actively move ahead trusting in His power, protection, and provision.

I have all kinds of mini monuments in my home office. A picture of my mentor and me. Several copies of a book (A *Tale of Three Kings* by Gene Edwards) that completely changed the trajectory of my life and ministry. A plumb line that reminds me that my heart needs to be in line with God's heart.

I'm staring right now at a brick that was taken from the demolition site of Beaver County Christian School in New Brighton, Pennsylvania. It reminds me how God intervened at a crucial time in high school and surrounded me with Christian men and women to speak God's truth into my rebellious and wandering heart.

I see two Pittsburgh Steelers footballs.

One football is from Vance, enscribed with a nice, personalized message. It reminds me of how God used him to redirect my ministry to make disciples of Jesus in and through the NFL.

The other is a game ball that Tomlin gave me. It's from the Pittsburgh Steelers vs. Buffalo Bills game at Highmark Stadium on September 12, 2021. The Steelers won that game 23–16. I did nothing to deserve a game ball, but it serves as a reminder of God's grace. I've done nothing to deserve it, but God gives it to me anyway, and I want to live every day letting people know they're eligible for God's team and His game ball of grace.

This is what mini monuments do. They help us to remember what God has done and cause us to live deliberately and intentionally for His purposes.

Do you have any that help you remember what God has done? If not, as you wait on the Lord, a good practice is to go back through your life and remember where God has intervened. Find a picture from that day. Go have a conversation with someone who was there, take a photo, and display it where you'll always see it. Create a mini monument from that significant moment to remind you of what God has done.

It strikes me as I write this section that the book you're holding in your hands now serves as a mini monument of what God has done in my life. I wrote it for you to be encouraged to follow Jesus into the unknown of your God-given purpose. I pray this book is a mini monument pointing you to God's power, protection, and provision for your journey ahead.

SECRET SERVING

One of the best ways to actively wait on the Lord is to serve Him and others in secret.

Serving God and His people helps reminds us of our ultimate purpose regardless of our vocation and/or destination.

It's not about you! Get your eyes off yourself and your traffic situation. Your ultimate God-given purpose will always involve you, but it will never be about you. It's always about God and other people. Get your eyes on Jesus and serve where you already know He wants you to serve. You don't have to pray about giving generously to your church. You don't have to wonder if God wants you to serve your neighbor. Look for a need and meet it. You don't have to guess if Jesus wants you to serve the poor, give food to the hungry, or visit the prisoner. Just go do it.

Go serve and keep your camera at home. Go on a mission trip with your church while you wait on God's direction for your life. Go serve in the nursery of your church. Go serve dinner at a homeless shelter. Go serve at the local food bank. Just go serve.

Tomlin says, "Get comfortable being uncomfortable." Take a risk and try something you know God has already called his Church to do. Keep your eyes and ears open to God's voice as you secretly serve in those spaces. I've discovered that it's often in the secret places of doing what God has already told us to do that God reveals more of Himself and His purposes for our lives.

Go ahead. Try it. Serve in secret. Do it afraid and watch what God does in you while you wait.

SPIRITUAL DISCIPLINES

One of the best ways to practice active waiting is through spiritual disciplines. We've discussed several of them already (prayer, reading God's Word), but I want to suggest one of the best books I've read on the topic.

Celebration of Discipline by Richard J. Foster is an incredible work on spiritual formation. Richard Foster explores spiritual practices for deeper personal transformation and maturity. He organizes these practices into three categories:

1. **Inward Disciplines** (Meditation, Prayer, Fasting, Study) for personal examination.
2. **Outward Disciplines** (Simplicity, Solitude, Submission, Service) for selfless engagement with the world.
3. **Corporate Disciplines** (Confession, Worship, Guidance, Celebration) for community and connection with God and others.

This book had an incredible impact on my life when I first read it as a young college student. God used it to form lifelong habits and spiritual rhythms in me that would draw me closer to Him in life, especially in the times of waiting.

Erica and I employed many of these spiritual disciplines as we considered the decision to jump on staff with AIA. While these were already a part of our regular rhythm, we ramped them up as we waited on the Lord. As you can see, the L.E.A.P. framework is largely a fresh perspective of these time-tested spiritual disciplines

PRAYER JOURNALING

There's journaling, and then there's prayer journaling. I knew about journaling, and I had sometimes written out my prayers to God as I journaled about my day or certain events. But this was next level, and I have to share it with you.

I traveled to Irvine, California to visit Mariners Church and be trained in a new discipleship experience called Rooted (experiencerooted.com). My church leadership decided to start this program while I was wrestling with my calling. I was waiting to hear back from Tomlin about the chaplain role, but nobody on the trip knew.

As a part of the Rooted experience, they trained us on how to guide people through a prayer experience. It's a prayer-focused combination of several spiritual disciplines. It's a powerful time of corporate and individual prayer. The prayer experience was phenomenal, but prayer journaling impacted me the most.

In prayer journaling, you read a passage of Scripture and write out your specific prayers according to what you just read, make observations, and then ask God questions and listen for His response. Praying out loud or in the quietness of your mind is powerful. I now believe it becomes even more powerful when you record what you're praying for in written form.

Here's why. As I read God's Word in Isaiah 43 and Ezekiel 37 that day in California, I wrote honestly about what I was feeling and asked God some crucial questions concerning His purpose for my life. I was communing with Him in writing. I took the time to be quiet and focus on His still small voice. I then wrote down what I felt God say to my heart in response to what I was writing. It was like a written invitation for God to come sit with me and speak to me through His Word.

What has become so powerful for me in prayer journaling is the date and timestamps. My "10:24 a.m. California Time" moment is written forever in my journal. This was huge for me as I waited on the Lord. On June 21, 2019, God clearly answered my cry and questions with the next step to move forward in pursuit of my God-given purpose and calling.

Throughout the years of journaling my prayers, I now have literal dates and timestamps where God has answered and how He's answered my prayers. This is not only powerful for me, but it will serve as mini monuments for future generations to know that God is alive and desires to speak to His children today.

I encourage you to start prayer journaling as you read God's Word. Ask Him questions.

Timestamp His answers and watch how this will grow your faith and confidence in His direction and timing.

Try it right now. Take the time to write down your prayers to God regarding what you just read in these last few pages.

God, what do you want me to do? Which one of these five ways of active waiting should I try first? Take the time and practice.

My prayer for you as you finish this chapter is that God will help you repurpose your wait through applying some of what I've written into your regular routine. I pray God will meet you in your traffic in a powerful way, and that it will give you the confidence that He is with you in the waiting. It's countercultural, but I pray that you will come to love waiting for the Lord. I pray for you to know that God is working in you and on you while you wait for Him to move you.

It's often in the waiting that God does His best work. If you let Him.

Now all I need you to do is let me know how God answered my prayer for you, so I can date it and timestamp it in my Prayer Journal. Seriously, I'd love to hear what God has done and is doing in your life. Please send your "Do It Afraid" story by visiting **doitafraidstories.com** when you have a moment.

CHAPTER 15

Yield to God's Call

*"The essence of surrender is getting out of God's way
so that He can do in us what He also wants to do through us."*
A. W. Tozer

"...not my will, but yours be done."
Luke 22:42

I loved the chaplain role and job description Tomlin offered me, but I didn't like the part of raising 100 percent of my salary, benefits, and ministry budget. There had to be another way, and I found it. Well, um... I created it. In fact, I produced two different ways this role could be done without me raising a ton of money, and I hoped Coach T would pick one of them.

A few days after I was offered the chaplain position, I went back to negotiate with Tomlin. I still can't believe I did that, but I did. This wasn't my best faith-filled moment. I almost didn't include this part of the story, but I feel compelled to be brutally honest about my lack of faith. I was afraid as I stood on top of the cliff. My "IOU" fear was holding me back from making the jump. I tried to figure out a way to get down to the water without taking the leap of faith.

I was confident in my preparation and presentation. I slid my two-solution proposal to him and asked if he would consider doing this another way. He didn't even look at the paper, and he firmly expressed that the role would only be offered through coming on staff with AIA. He explained his loyalty to and appreciation for AIA, and the importance of this role having a covering organization and brotherhood of chaplains for wisdom and accountability. I understood his position and appreciated his reasoning, but I still didn't like the fundraising part.

I had a massive decision to make.

Would I go all in? Would I surrender to God's call on His terms, or would I walk away from it? Would I relinquish trying to find a way to make this work on my terms, or would I submit to God's way and make the leap of faith?

CORE CONVICTION

I have a core conviction when it comes to God's call.

God doesn't ask. God commands.

As I search the Scriptures, I have not found a time where God asks somebody to do something. Would you be willing? When you get a moment, could you? If you don't mind, can you?

No! God always commands. God directs. God tells. God orders.

Genesis 2:16 — And the LORD God commanded the man... Genesis 6:13 — God said to Noah, "...make yourself an ark..."

Genesis 12:1 — The Lord had said to Abram, "Go from your country, your people and your father's household to the land I will show you."

Genesis 26:2-3 — The Lord appeared to Isaac and said, "...Stay in this land..."

Genesis 46:10 — God spoke to Jacob, "Do not be afraid to go down to Egypt, for I will make you into a great nation there."

Exodus 3:10 — God spoke to Moses, "So now, go. I am sending you to Pharaoh to bring my people the Israelites out of Egypt."

Joshua 3:7-8 — And the Lord said to Joshua, "Tell the priests who carry the ark of the covenant: '...go and stand in the river.'"

I could keep going through the Old Testament, but by now you're getting my point. God commands. He doesn't ask.

What about Jesus? Does he ask? No.

Throughout the Gospels, we see Jesus engaging in conversation with people and asking great questions, but he always directs the conversation with an authoritative command. Go and sin no more. Come and see. Follow me. Get up, take your mat, and go home. Take the log out of your own eye. Do not worry. Come to me, all you who are weary and burdened.

Even Jesus' invitations are commands to be followed. He didn't ask the disciples if they wanted to follow. Yes, it was an invitational command, but it was always an invitation on His clear terms. It wasn't up for a debate.

Ultimate Authority leaves no room for negotiation.

LORDSHIP

Knowing all this, I still tried to negotiate with God and Tomlin. It didn't go well. It never does. I should know better by now.

We don't have the right to negotiate with God. He's God! He is the Ultimate Authority. He is the LORD, and we will always find ourselves heading toward trouble when we try to strike a deal or find a middle ground with Him. When it comes to God's call on our lives, He does not waver. When it comes to His will for our lives, He does not negotiate. He expects us to obey and obey Him right away.

Why?

Because He's God. Because He's good. Because He cares for us and those we care for.

Because He knows His way is always the best way. Because He always wants what is best for us.

While God does not negotiate, He still gives you the freedom to choose His best. He will never force you to choose Him or His will for your life. You can either surrender to His way or walk away. You have the choice to follow Him into His will for your life or follow your heart into your own will.

God's purpose and will for your life is not up for debate, but you do have a choice to make.

Will you make Jesus the Lord of your decisions? Will you surrender your whole life to His leadership? Will you relinquish your rights and serve Him as your Master? Will you submit to God's complete control?

Jesus is either Lord of all, or He's not Lord at all. Either He's in charge, or you're in charge. There's no middle ground. It's His command. It's His invitation. It's God's best. Take it or leave it.

GOD, ARE YOU TELLING ME TO JUMP?

I trust that if you've read this far in this book that you want to do what God is telling you to do. You're just trying to figure out how to do it or if it's really God who is speaking.

How do you know if you're supposed to jump? How do you know if what you're sensing is God's call to jump into God-given purpose? Where is God telling you to go? When is God telling you jump? How do you know it's God speaking and not your imagination or someone else's opinion?

I want to share with you a game changer that will boost your confidence in hearing the voice of God. With his permission, this is a literal page out of my mentor's book A *Discipleship Journey*. Dave writes the following in his chapter, "Hearing the Voice of God."

> We can and should expect to hear God speak to us, as the Scriptures remind us that the sheep hear the Shepherd's voice (John 10:3–4, 27). But how can we know when it is really God and not our own thoughts and imaginations? We should test what we hear, as the Scriptures encourage us to do (Rom 12:2; 1 Thes. 5:21; 1 John 4:1–3).
>
> Here are some confirming questions you can ask:
>
> **Is It Biblical?**
>
> The Holy Spirit will *never* ask us to do something that is contrary to the Scriptures. He will never violate the value of people that Jesus has died for, nor will He lead someone to do something outside the biblical attitude of walking well under authority.
>
> **Is It in Line with God's Character and Ways?**
>
> God cannot contradict who He is. He will not ask us to do something that opposes His character and ways as revealed in the Scriptures.
>
> **Does It Glorify Jesus and Draw People Closer to Him?**
>
> God will not ask us to walk outside of love or do something that will communicate a distorted image of Himself to others.

Does It Bear Witness to You?

As you consider stepping into what you believe God asked you to do, do you sense the Holy Spirit affirming this within you? Is there peace? Is there a sense of faith, hope, and courage that accompanies God's direction to you?

Does It Bear Witness to Other Believers with Whom You Walk Closely?

Do others around you and those with whom you walk closest confirm your hearing from God? When you ask for advice, what do those who provide spiritual leadership in your life say?

Apply the Triple Confirmation to Confirm God's Leading

Does it align with the Bible?

Does the Holy Spirit bear witness within you?

What has God said to you through other believers and your spiritual leaders?

Think of the Triple Confirmation as a series of three traffic lights. If what you are sensing aligns with the Bible, then it's green and safe to move forward. If the Holy Spirit is nudging you to move and providing you peace, then it's green and you can proceed. If what others are saying to you lines up with God's Word and affirming God's direction, then that light is green, and you can move forward with confidence.

If they're all green, GO!

Remember, God desires to speak to you! Don't make this more complicated for yourself. God wants to get you where He desires for you to go, and He'll protect you from driving into places He doesn't want you to go. The Holy Spirit is good at positioning a yellow light or a red light.

As you're practicing the L.E.A.P posture, He'll give you plenty of signs along the road. If you've surrendered the wheel to Jesus, and given up any rights to take it back, then you can trust that the green lights are confirming God's voice to move ahead.

YIELD

Even with the Triple Confirmation, I realize that it can still be scary to jump into your God-given purpose. Fear begins to take hold and competes against God's command. The enemy of your soul wants to downplay God's authority. Logic begins to creep in and rationalize your excuses. Other people tell you not to jump. There are so many competing voices that continue to hold you back.

It's a wrestling match at the top of that cliff. You know you want to do it. You know you're supposed to do it. You can feel it in your gut. You dream about it. You can't shake God's call.

You think about it in your free time. If you had all the money in the world, you would do it. You may have even gone so far as to create a plan for it. You know God is commanding you to do it, and you'd love to jump, but...

There's something still holding you back. Keeping you at the top of the cliff.

A comfortable lifestyle. A family to provide for. A friend's strong opinion. A good position at work. A solid paycheck.

And I get it. I've been there. I understand completely. These are legitimate concerns.

However, in this final chapter, I want to challenge you in the same way God confronted Erica and me. I want to encourage you to count the severe cost of staying on top of the cliff and not jumping into God's call on your life.

I want to be careful to write this next part so that it comes across gentle yet firm while hoping that you know my heart is for you.

None of those people or things are Lord of your life. Jesus is Lord of your life.

Either Jesus is Lord, or your family is.

Either Jesus is Lord, or your paycheck is.

Either Jesus is Lord, or your position is.

Either Jesus is Lord, or your house is.

As long as you stay on top of that cliff and dig in your heels, you are being disobedient to Jesus' Lordship over all aspects of your life. And you make a lousy Lord. So do I.

Who are you to negotiate with the Living God? Do you really want to stand before God one day and give your excuses as to why you didn't obey His command?

Remember, what God has revealed is not meant to be negotiated. It's meant to be obeyed. Delayed obedience is disobedience.

Negotiation with God is disobedience.

Once Erica and I realized that our negotiation with Tomlin was actually disobedience to God, we had to repent and ask for His forgiveness. We knew that we were supposed to trust Him with everything, and we were holding back and trying to manipulate the situation on our terms.

God was not asking if we wanted to do this. God was commanding us to do this. His way.

We finally yielded. We relinquished any rights to His direct orders. We submitted ourselves to His call and we did it fearing the Lord of our marriage, family, and ministry. We surrendered all, and we took the leap of faith.

Are you being disobedient to God's command? Do you need to repent and ask God for forgiveness? Are you holding anything back from His Lordship?

I invite you to put this book down, and yield everything to God's call. No more negotiating. It's time to obey.

Do it afraid.

Conclusion

CONCLUSION

Imagine yourself at the top of that cliff in the Adirondacks. You so badly want to jump, but your brain is convincing you it's not safe. As you peer over the edge, you can see me at the bottom showing you exactly where to jump. I'm down there cheering you on. I was just like you a moment ago, but I decided to embrace the fear of the unknown, and I hit that narrow landing zone. You can see the exhilaration on my face!

Now it's your turn.

You can do this!

Don't let fear steal this moment.

Don't let fear rob you of all that God has for you.

I want you to know and experience the adventure God is calling you to and the purpose for which He has created you to live. But here's the thing… it will require you to embrace the fear of the unknown and take that leap of faith. Trust God. Follow Jesus' example. Hit that narrow landing zone where God's call meets your obedience to jump and trust Him with your life.

Trust me! You will come alive in ways beyond your imagination. C'mon!

Do it afraid!

SHARE YOUR STORY

Erica and I would love to hear your "Do It Afraid" story! We are in this journey with you, and we'd love to join your jump like you've joined ours. Would you consider visiting **doitafraidstories.com** and sharing your story with us? We'd love to cheer you on!

Acknowledgments

FIRST AND FOREMOST, I want to thank and deflect the glory to Jesus Christ. Without You, I am nothing, and I wouldn't have a God-story to share. You called me to serve God as a young man, and You gave me this and every opportunity. Thank you for your guidance and provision in my life.

ERICA — Thank you for jumping with me into this adventure of marriage, family, and ministry. Look at what God has done! You are my closest confidant. I love you. I love the life God has built for us. I love following Jesus with you. Here's to Team Chevalier!

MADALYN, KALEA, AND AINSLEY — Each of you make me so proud! I love being your dad! One of God's greatest gifts to me is watching you chase Jesus in your own unique ways. You've lived this story with Mom and me, and I cannot wait to see how God continues to write your stories as you jump with Him in the years ahead.

MY PARENTS — My dad won't get to read this book because he's in Heaven now, but Mom... thank you for everything growing up, especially having the foresight to work at Geneva College, which allowed me to have a free college education. I was able to grow in my faith there and surrender my life to God's call of ministry. Your resilience and sacrifice are a motivation for me.

DAVE BUEHRING — You are a spiritual father to me. Your influence in my life is all over the pages of this book and those God has allowed me to influence. Your words are big in my ears. Thank you for modeling and challenging me to make disciple makers to the third and fourth generations.

RANDY TOMKO—Thank you for showing me a different way to do ministry. I always describe our season with you and Rockpointe as rescuing our marriage from ministry. I will be forever grateful that God crossed my leadership path with yours.

SCOTT STEVENS—Thank you for coming alongside me when I was a young youth pastor. Thanks for keeping tabs on me when I left Pittsburgh for a while and inviting me to join staff at North Way. As my pastor and boss at the time, you allowed me to explore the opportunity with the Steelers. You created a safe place for me to wrestle with my calling while I was still a part of your staff. I will be forever grateful for you and North Way.

BEN KENDREW—Before we could walk or talk, we've been best friends. We've been through a lot together. Thanks for being the kind of friend that will get in my face to hold me accountable to the Jesus Standard. What I love most about our friendship is that we've encouraged each other to become the "Standard Bearers" for future generations that will follow us. Frodo and Sam to the end!

VINCE AND LARI LOCHER—Thank you for being a mentor couple to Erica and me. Thank you for allowing us to run this decision (and many more) past you and always pointing us to Jesus. Your wisdom on marriage and parenting is invaluable to us.

BRAD AND BETH HENDERSON—Your marriage, parenting, and ministry has been a model that Erica and I have wanted to emulate. Your experience as the Pittsburgh Pirates and Penguins chaplains helped prepare us to jump into NFL Chaplaincy. Your leadership of the Pittsburgh Kids Foundation has impacted our family for generations to come.

VANCE MCDONALD—God used you to change the trajectory of my life and ministry. You introduced me to this whole adventure! Thank you for opening the door.

MIKE TOMLIN—Thank you for taking a risk on me and giving me the opportunity to stretch my faith in ways I didn't know it needed to be stretched. Your leadership has deeply impacted me, and I appreciate how you value the chaplain position for the men and women of the Steelers organization.

OUR MINISTRY PARTNERS—Without you, Erica and I would not be able to do what we do. Thank you for prayerfully and financially partnering with us in this ministry.

ABOUT THE
Author

Kent Chevalier is an inspirational speaker and author known for his passion for leadership, purpose, and faith. His talks have encouraged countless lives across CEO forums, YPO chapters, real estate firms, banking and restaurant industries, and the transportation sector. Kent has also spoken to teams throughout the NCAA and the NFL.

After two decades serving in various pastoral leadership roles in the local Church context, Kent was invited by Pittsburgh Steelers Head Coach, Mike Tomlin, to serve as an NFL chaplain in 2019. He now speaks at different universities, churches, businesses, and conferences across the United States.

Kent is also the founder of the *Deflect the Glory*™ movement that raises awareness and resources for nonprofit ministries in Pittsburgh, Pennsylvania.

He earned a bachelor's degree in student ministry from Geneva College and a master's degree in theological studies from Trinity Evangelical Divinity School.

Kent is from Pittsburgh and he values most being a husband to Erica and a dad to their three adult daughters and one son-in-law.

Book Kent Chevalier

TO SPEAK WITH YOUR TEAM, PROGRAM, OR ORGANIZATION

For speaking inquiries, submit a request at
kentchevalier.com.

Stay Connected

WITH KENT CHEVALIER ON SOCIAL MEDIA

 kentchevalier   kentchevalier   kent.chevalier.5

Representing a community of authors whose books have collectively sold hundreds of millions of copies, the founders of The Gray + Miller Agency launched Maison Vero, a professional publishing house that partners with rising authors to bring their thought leadership to the world. Our representation covers every aspect of thought leadership, including U.S. senators, governors, and ambassadors, billionaire founders and entrepreneurs, researchers, academics, scientists, consultants, practitioners, social influencers, C-suite leaders, adventurers, professional athletes, artists, and creators. We partner with thought leaders and world changers like you who have a story to tell. By bringing decades of professional expertise to our clients, we are charting a new path in a timeless industry that transcends publishing norms, transforming powerful thoughts into impactful books that inspire minds, ignite hearts, and open doors.

Visit maisonvero.com to view our growing list of authors, or to submit a proposal for publication consideration.

Follow Maison Vero for insight and inspiration on social media:

 MaisonVero   MaisonVero   MaisonVeroPublishing

For information about special discounts for bulk purchases, please call (949) 333-4872 or email info@graymilleragency.com.

Maison Vero is a partner brand of The Gray + Miller Agency, a speaking, literary, and talent consortium. For more information on the talent represented by The Gray + Miller Agency, or to bring any of our thought leaders to your organization or live event, please visit our website at graymilleragency.com.

www.ingramcontent.com/pod-product-compliance
Lightning Source LLC
LaVergne TN
LVHW040057080526
838202LV00045B/3685